High Availability

Successful Implementation for the Data-driven Enterprise

A technical guide from the experts at Perpetual Technologies, Inc.

Published by Perpetual Publications, an affiliate of Perpetual Technologies, Inc.

9155 Harrison Park Court

Indianapolis, IN 46216

(800)538-0453

www.perptech.com

HIGH AVAILABILITY

SUCCESSFUL IMPLEMENTATION FOR THE DATA-DRIVEN ENTERPRISE

Copyright © 2007 by Perpetual Publications, Inc.

All rights reserved. No part of this book shall be reproduced, stored in a retrieval system, or transmitted by any means, electronic, mechanical, photocopying, recording, or otherwise, without written permission from the publisher. No patent liability is assumed with respect to the use of information contained herein. Although every precaution has been taken in the preparation of this book, the publisher and author assume no responsibility for errors or omissions. Neither is any liability assumed for damages resulting from the use of the information contained herein.

International Standard Book Number: 0-9786055-0-0

Printed in the United States of America

First Printing: January 2007

Trademarks

Many of the terms used by manufacturers and sellers to distinguish their products are claimed as trademarks. Where those terms are mentioned in this book and are known to be trademarks or service marks, the terms have been appropriately capitalized. While every precaution has been made during the preparation of this book, Perpetual Publications cannot attest to the accuracy of this information. Use of a term in this book should not be regarded as affecting the validity of any trademark or service mark.

Warning and Disclaimer

Every effort has been made to make this book as complete and as accurate as possible, but no warranty or fitness is implied. The information provided is on an "as is" basis. The authors and the publisher shall have neither liability nor responsibility to any person or entity with respect to any loss or damages arising from the information contained in this book.

Primary Authors	Contributing Authors	Editors	Reviewers
Mike Wessler	Dan Wilson	Sarah Hines	Angie Gleim
Ryan Stephens	Chris Sarjent	Ryan Stephens	Ron Plew
Chris Zeis	John Price	John Price	Bob Garrett
	Brian Conant	Amy Jo Putz	

CONCEPTS YOU WILL LEARN IN THIS BOOK

	Page
• Understanding high availability (HA)	4
• Eliminating single points of failure	5
• Clustering hardware for redundancy	15
• Selecting the best operating systems	21
• Establishing secondary database environments for failover	32
• Clustering database environments for redundancy and performance	36
• Collaboration between web and application servers	47
• Clustered and redundant web application environments	49
• Network and Internet load balancing	54
• Network security and its impact on HA environments	64
• Management methodologies that support HA	71
• Personnel requirements to support an HA project	75
• Developing a Disaster Recovery Plan (DRP)	83
• Balancing budget and HA requirements	96
• Identifying systems that are most critical	99
• Mitigating risks associated with unavailability	103
• Industry regulatory issues and their impact on HA systems	113
• Emerging HA technologies	117
• Avoiding common mistakes during HA implementation	121

CONTENTS

Acknowledgments *1*

Foreword *2*

Chapter 1: Introduction to High Availability *4*
   Single Point of Failure 5
   Causes of Unavailability 7
   Determining Required Availability 8
   Identifying Critical Systems 9
   The SLA in HA 10
   Managing HA 10
   Requirements for Successful HA Implementation 10

Chapter 2: Hardware, Storage Management, and Operating Systems. *13*
   Basic Server Hardware Considerations 14
   Hardware Cluster Architecture 15
   Storage Management 19
   Operating Systems 21

Chapter 3: Databases *26*
   Dynamics of the Database 27
   Inadequacy of Traditional Backup and Recovery 28
   Secondary Database Environments 32
   Clustered Database Environments 36
   Managing Memory Synchronization 38

Chapter 4: Web and Application Servers *45*
   Role of the Web Server 45
   Role of the Application Server 46
   How Web and Application Servers Work Together 47
   Redundant Web Application Servers 49
   Clustered Web Application Servers 51
   Network Load Balancing Options 54

Complete HA Implementation 56

Chapter 5: Networking 59

Highly Available Networks 59
Network HA Concepts 59
Internet Connectivity 60
Routing and Switching 62
Firewalls and Network Security 64
DNS 67
Network Management 68

Chapter 6: Employing and Managing HA 71

Methodologies to Employ and Manage HA 71
Other Management Models that Support HA 74
Qualifications of Personnel to Support HA 75
Implementing HA 77
Managing HA 78
Communication, Knowledge Transfer, and Transition 80
Documentation 81

Chapter 7: Disaster Recovery Planning 83

Types of Disasters 84
Develop the DRP Objectives 86
DRP Development 87
Develop the Technical Plan 89
Implement the Plan 92
Test the Recovery 94

Chapter 8: Balancing the Budget and HA 96

Stakeholder Buy In 97
Meeting Minimum Requirements 98
Consequences to Consider 101
Mitigating Risk 103
Associating Unavailability with Cost 105

Example 1: Inability to Make and Ship Widgets 105
Example 2: Unavailability of Web and E-commerce 106
Example 3: The Importance of Email 107
Example 4: Financial Impact on Development Operations 108
HA Accountability and ROI 110
Worksheets to Help Balance HA With Budget 110

Chapter 9: HA and Regulatory Compliance 113

Chapter 10: The Future of HA 117
Distributed Computing 117
Parallel Computing 117
On-Demand Computing 118
Grid Computing 118

Chapter 11: Common Mistakes 121
Common Misconceptions 122
Common Mistakes 124

Appendix A: List of Acronyms 132

Appendix B: Service Level Agreement Checklist 134

Appendix C: Service Level Agreement Outline 136

Appendix D: Single Point of Failure Checklist 138

Appendix E: Disaster Recovery Plan Checklist 140

Glossary 144

Index 150

Other Books by Perpetual Technologies' Experts 156

ACKNOWLEDGMENTS

Turning the mere idea of this book into a finished product turned out to be much more work than our team anticipated. As with any book we have written, it required strong collaboration. First, I would like to thank the Perpetual Technologies team, whose experience became the source of knowledge for this book. An IT service provider is nothing without its people, and we have some of the best. I want to thank Mike Wessler for stepping up to the plate and taking project ownership by delivering the largest portion of this book's content. Thanks to the other authors who invested extra time outside of their daily technical duties to provide valuable material: Chris Zeis, Dan Wilson, Chris Sarjent, John Price, and Brian Conant. Several individuals provided valuable input in the early stages of development; they are Amy Merfeld, Larry Patterson, and Brad Severance. Thank you. In the final stages, editing became a major undertaking. First, I thank John Price for accepting this task and providing quick turnaround. Second, I thank Sarah Hines for going through this entire book with a fine-tooth comb and taking great pride in her work to maximize the quality of this book. Third, the efforts of Ron Plew and Leigh Mulroy were instrumental in preparing the book for production. Before concluding, I must express my appreciation for the confidence our clients place in Perpetual Technologies; I am confident this book will help organizations be more proactive in maintaining highly available information systems. Whether partner, employee, customer, or affiliate, I am honored by all the individuals that have an impact on Perpetual Technologies, while we continually strive to achieve higher standards for the data-driven enterprise.

Ryan Stephens
President and CEO
Perpetual Technologies, Inc.

Foreword

In today's marketplace, competitive advantage relies on availability of data. Reliance on data is like quicksand, in that each day we get deeper and deeper as technology progresses. Data never shrinks but always grows, making information systems more difficult to manage and critical to maintain.

Operational efficiency and client satisfaction are directly related to the performance and functionality of technologies. With a vast array of solutions to choose from, it is essential that companies evaluate the pros and cons of each. This book is intended to provide a detailed overview of high availability (HA) concepts and options. An HA solution is one that ensures maximum uptime of your critical systems to increase the effectiveness of your organization and decrease the risks associated with unplanned system downtime.

With experience in providing mission-critical database and information systems support, our team has witnessed the power of properly-employed technology and the devastating effect of poorly chosen solutions. Investing in a product without fully understanding its capabilities is a common error that our technical team observes on a weekly basis. Understanding the benefits and risks of technology is the first step in successfully implementing a solution.

Lack of system availability affects all levels of an organization. With that in mind, this book was written for executive management, IT management, and technicians. The material included herein contains concepts, options, resources, case studies, and detailed technical information to serve as a resource in finding the right blend of HA solutions for your company.

For your convenience, the following icons are provided throughout the book. Each icon contains valuable thoughts and/or real-world examples of lessons learned.

Notes are included throughout to emphasize important points.

Case studies are provided based on real-world situations.

A reflection section is included at the end of each chapter to help you immediately apply important concepts covered.

Additional resources are included in the back of the book as appendices. These resources are provided for use to help with HA planning for any organization.

- Appendix A – Acronyms Used in This Book
- Appendix B – Service Level Agreement Checklist
- Appendix C – Sample Service Level Agreement
- Appendix D – Single Point of Failure Checklist
- Appendix E – Disaster Recovery Plan Checklist
- Glossary

We are confident you will find this book useful, and thank you for using Perpetual Technologies as a resource for evaluating your HA needs.

Perpetual Technologies' Team
www.perptech.com

CHAPTER 1: INTRODUCTION TO HIGH AVAILABILITY

We live in a data-driven world. Critical information must be at the fingertips of customers, managers, and end users. Small fortunes are invested in sophisticated information systems with too little emphasis placed on guaranteed availability, which is one of the most fundamental and single-most important concerns of an IT department. Management and customers hold IT accountable for availability above all. Figure 1.1 illustrates the integration between people and data system components that has become so critical in the modern data-driven culture.

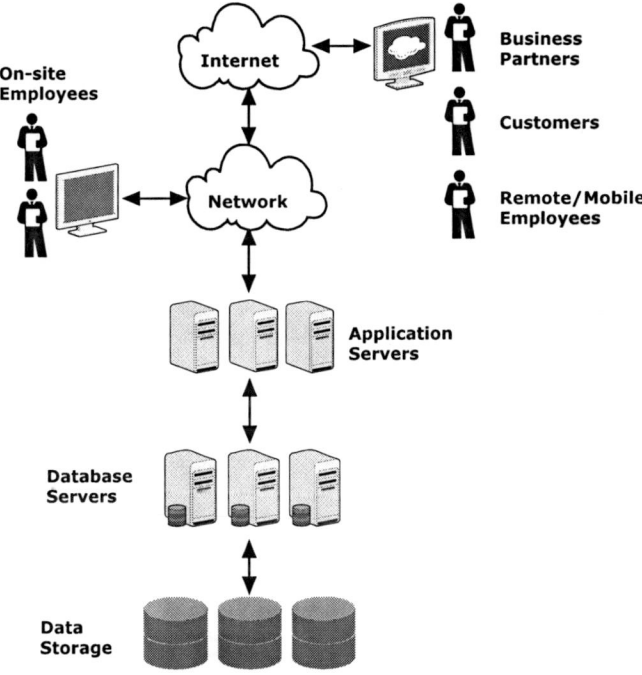

Figure 1.1   Integration of people and data systems

Imagine the frustration of a customer trying to access personal account information when the system is down. Imagine the embarrassment of a senior executive in the middle of a briefing to a high profile customer when the system fails. IT is often measured not by its successes but by its failures. Availability is a simple concept but poses a serious threat to any organization.

What is the cost of losing sales or customers? What is the cost associated with an unavailable critical system? For example, suppose you have 50 medical claims processors and the average cost of each is $35 per hour including overhead. If the system is down for four hours, loss of labor productivity costs the organization $7,000; not to mention, missed deadlines, lack of responsiveness to customers, and other related costs will occur. When data is not available, customers cannot place orders, management cannot make decisions, inventory cannot be replenished, payroll cannot be processed, communication fails, and customer relationships are strained.

NOTE
Customers and end users hold the system's management team and vendors accountable for availability more than any other technical issue. Even if a system component is fully available, the perception of downtime is the same as actual downtime to a client.

Highly available systems guarantee a certain level of critical data availability. The term "high" is relative, and the level of guarantee is specific to each organization. HA is guaranteed through redundancy. Hardware and software solutions exist to facilitate a custom level of redundancy.

Single Point of Failure

A single point of failure is a single avenue from one system component to another. If removed, unavailability occurs. For mission-critical information systems, it is important to identify all possible single points of failure. Once identified, the single point of failure should be addressed. Planning and building an HA environment around single points of failure will help reduce the risk of unavailability. For example, if you have a power failure and no backup power source, then the result will be unavailability of all systems. In this case, the power supply is the single point of failure. Let's say you install battery backups or a generator in case of power loss. If your main power source is lost, the secondary power source will keep your systems available. Consequently, your power source is no longer a single point of failure. This holds true for network connections, hardware, software, databases, applications, and any other system components with dependencies.

Figure 1.2 shows how one single point of failure can be eliminated in a basic eCommerce environment. By having a secondary network avenue into the eCommerce site, customers can still purchase goods if the primary network is unavailable. Once this single point of failure is handled, the unavailability of one Internet connection would be transparent to the customer and transactions should continue.

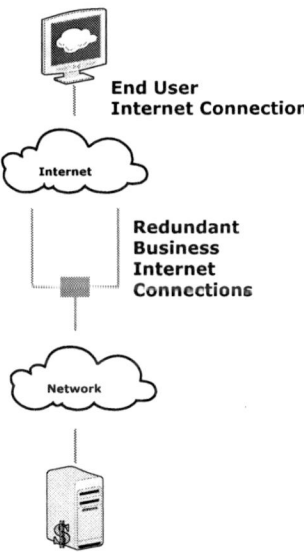

Figure 1.2   **Single Point of Failure Eliminated**

Throughout this book, we'll take a deeper look into all the major system components to help evaluate single points of failure. All organizations require different standards for an HA environment; therefore, the first step is to understand the risks and consequences associated with unavailability.

Causes of Unavailability

There are two categories of unavailability: scheduled downtime and unscheduled downtime. Scheduled downtime usually involves some form of system maintenance such as patching, upgrading, tuning, and system backup processing. Unscheduled downtime can be caused by things such as system failure, power failure, natural disaster, and user error. Since unscheduled system downtime is unpredictable, a contingency plan must exist.

A contingency plan for unscheduled downtime should, at a minimum, address the following issues:

- What are the consequences of system unavailability?
- How will the organization continue to operate?
- How will data be recovered?
- How will systems be revived?
- Who will recover the data?
- What is the expected recovery time?
- What systems are critical to the organization?
- When is system availability most critical?
- What HA options are available?
- What HA options, if any, will be implemented?
- How will your HA solution be managed?
- What budgetary constraints exist?

NOTE High availability planning is all about contingency planning. Inevitably, your system will experience downtime. Some downtime is predictable and some is not. It is important to study the behavior of your system, how various components within your system are integrated, and how users utilize your system. With a solid understanding of your system environment and your organization's mission, it is easier to anticipate threats and devise a contingency plan that will maximize availability when problems occur outside of your control.

Determining Required Availability

Absolute availability is not possible, no matter how much you spend. Table 1.1 displays universal standards for availability based on percentage of uptime. While 99% uptime may be acceptable for one organization, it could destroy a company that can't afford two business weeks of downtime per year.

Table 1.1   Availability by Percentage

Availability	Allowable downtime per year	Allowable downtime per day
99%	87.6 hours (2 business weeks)	14.4 minutes
99.5%	43.8 hours (1 business week)	7.2 minutes
99.9%	8.76 hours (1 business day)	1.44 minutes
99.99%	0.85 hours (1 business hour)	0.14 minutes (8.4 seconds)
100%	0 hours	0 minutes

Operating hours play an important role in HA. When do internal users access systems? When do customers expect to have access? When does your heaviest system traffic occur? Can your system be taken down for maintenance without any impact? If not, what time windows have the least amount of impact on users?

Table 1.2 shows common operating-hour groupings to consider in HA planning. Many organizations do not have personnel to support the level of availability that is needed. For this reason, remote administration has become a popular alternative. If outsourcing administration is a justifiable option, vendors will need to know which level of support is needed based on the following groupings.

Table 1.2   Common Operating Hours

Common Operating Hours
Normal business hours (i.e. 8am – 5pm), Monday - Friday
Extended business hours (i.e. 6am – 9pm), Monday - Friday
7 days per week with typical work hours
24/7 not including weekends and holidays
24/7 including weekends and holidays

Other factors to consider concerning operating hours are:

- Systems with end users worldwide with 24/7 access
- Organizations with locations in multiple time zones
- Organizations with customers in multiple time zones
- Depth of staff to support systems and HA solution

Identifying Critical Systems

It is common to desire availability of all systems at all times; however, the reality is that some are critical and others demand little or no attention when unavailable during certain times. Some systems support customers and have a direct impact on revenue. The most critical systems should be the first focus of an HA plan and have the majority of the budget.

The SLA in HA

A service level agreement (SLA) is a document that outlines the levels of systems support necessary to meet business needs and how performance will be measured. An SLA may be utilized internally or externally. Internally, the document creates accountability for the IT department, and an external SLA defines deliverables promised by a vendor. Every organization should require a service level agreement to support HA. A properly written SLA clearly defines critical systems, how they will be supported, when they are expected to be available, and what the consequences will be for non-compliance. Your HA solution should be built around your SLA. Whether your systems are being supported internally or by a third party, an SLA is important to ensure high availability and adequate support.

Managing HA

Ensuring proper success of an HA solution requires the capability to plan, implement, and manage an HA solution. Many plans are implemented but never tested. In fact, many organizations do not have a basic backup and recovery plan or the confidence to ensure availability or recovery of systems. A disaster recovery plan (DRP) is still a foreign concept to many organizations. To those that are familiar, the DRP is often a shot in the dark, or a blind-grasp attempt to recover as much data as possible. If a disaster recovery plan has not been established, documented, and successfully tested, an HA plan alone will be worthless in the event of a disaster.

Requirements for Successful HA Implementation

There are many requirements for successful HA implementation. Table 1.3 provides a basic description of the major requirements.

Table 1.3   Requirements for HA Implementation

HA Element	Requirements
People	HA solutions are challenging to implement and require knowledgeable and capable people. Whether internal or external, adequate staff is required to manage and implement an HA solution.
Stakeholder buy-in	Stakeholders must buy into your HA solution, because manpower and capital may be required to implement it. Depending on what is required, stakeholders may include the CEO, CIO, CFO, IT staff, end users, and customers.
Hardware	Some HA solutions require special hardware.
Software	Some HA solutions require special software.
Redundancy	Redundancy is crucial to HA. Components requiring redundancy may include power supply (backup generators, batteries), network, systems, databases, applications, and other related components. Hardware and software provide redundancy.
Backups	Successful backups are essential when considering an HA solution. Data availability and recoverability cannot be guaranteed without good backups.
Disaster Recovery Plan	Regardless of the amount of an HA investment, lack of a DRP can lead to complete loss of business data and failures.
Ongoing management	All HA solutions require ongoing management. The extent of the solution depends on size and complexity.
Periodic testing	Backup and recovery procedures along with DRPs should be tested periodically. Testing provides an opportunity to train staff and ensure proper implementation of procedures if unavailability would occur.
Adaptation	As business and system requirements change, HA solutions need to adapt. Failing to adapt could result in loss of investment.

Organizations struggle with HA for the following reasons:

- Budgetary constraints
- Lack of knowledge within the department
- Lack of stakeholder buy-in
- Lack of understanding of system and business requirements
- Basic implementation of systems

**CHAPTER 1
REFLECTION**

Availability is the single most important expectation by system users and customers. Reliability, performance, and immediate access to needed information create direct and indirect impacts on revenue, productivity, and customer retention.

Take a few minutes to reflect on the following thoughts to help formulate ways to make your systems more highly available.

1. What information drives the purpose of your system and comprises the core of your organization?

2. What is your most mission-critical system?

3. What single points of failure exist in your system environment?

4. How does HA affect both external and internal customers? What about the impact to your customers' customers?

5. How would system unavailability affect internal operations of your organization?

6. When is the last time you verified the existence and accuracy of your backup and recovery procedure? What pieces are missing to transform your recoverable system into a highly available system?

7. Do you have a Service Level Agreement (SLA) in place? If so, does it need to be revisited to address HA concerns?

CHAPTER 2: HARDWARE, STORAGE MANAGEMENT, AND OPERATING SYSTEMS

Anyone who has ever built or worked on a personal computer can tell you the key components are the Central Processing Unit (CPU), memory, disk, and operating system. Each piece has its job and countless options and configurations are available. Technicians should weigh the options for each component and assemble the right mix to meet the current need as well as future needs due to growth. The same principles apply when building HA servers that support an organization. This chapter discusses the necessary components for an effective HA solution.

To achieve true HA, hardware and software components must be combined together so single points of failure do not exist. Hardware needs to have redundant power supplies, hot replaceable components (disks), and the ability to lose a component and still operate. A hot replaceable component is a component that can be replaced immediately without taking down the system. The goal is to construct a system that has a high level of operation and very little time spent on unplanned outages. While the combination of hardware and software can provide redundancy with no single point of failure, an HA system is not necessarily designed to provide continuous uptime. In an HA system, an application can experience a failure due to hardware or software. A properly-designed HA system allows the application to return to production in a matter of minutes instead of hours or, in extreme cases, days. Decision makers should keep in mind that reliability measures the system's ability to function continuously, and availability is the system's ability to meet the organization's Service Level Agreements (SLA).

NOTE
When negotiating an SLA with your customers, make sure the SLAs with your own vendors' support the level of service to which you are committing. It is even common for IT service providers to have SLAs from third parties such as hardware vendors and Internet service providers.

For most environments, a high availability solution is ideal. Many businesses can accommodate a system failure that has a short recovery window; however, businesses that would suffer a huge financial loss need a higher level of reliability and availability. A fault-tolerant solution is required for these environments. Decision makers must keep in mind that fault tolerance will do nothing to prevent an application and software failure but can keep the system up despite a failure of an individual component.

Basic Server Hardware Considerations

When selecting and configuring server hardware, it is common practice to review performance characteristics. System administrators should know how fast the CPU is, the type of chip, and whether or not it possesses dual core technology. Memory and disk storage should also be considered for performance and HA capability.

A server with the fastest CPU on the market does nothing for an organization if that single CPU burns out. Many small Windows and Linux servers (and even entry-level UNIX servers) often come with only one CPU. Clearly these are not suitable for an HA system if that one server is critical. For fault-tolerance and performance reasons, it is important to have multiple CPUs per server when possible. Multiple processor servers typically come with even numbers of CPUs (e.g. 2, 4, 8.) Even if one CPU fails, or begins to fail, the server can still continue to process the work, even at a reduced rate, rather than being completely disabled.

Memory is critical to any server, especially application and database servers. Too little memory forces paging and swapping which can doom performance for any system. Additionally, as memory cards may fail, having extra memory in a server can keep a server available. Implementing the use of multiple memory cards may assist in a healthier HA solution.

Hard drives should be mirrored where possible, particularly when supporting key components such as the root file system that is necessary for any server. Mirroring a drive physically means having an exact duplicate of the production database. Many systems have failed because someone forgot to mirror a root drive and the disk failed. These mistakes are easy to make, because mirroring is often overlooked. Severe costs due to unavailability may be associated with this error; therefore, it is important for the system administrator to select and configure server components that are fault tolerant.

After server configuration needs have been identified, built, and delivered, pay specific attention to the maintenance plan and backup response time. Especially with larger and more complex servers, the vendor may be contractually tasked with supplying replacement hardware parts and installing them. Vendors should understand the SLA and be able to respond in an acceptable timeframe if server components fail. It is unfortunate when system recoveries are delayed because replacement parts have to be special ordered. For this reason, consider storing commonly needed spare parts onsite; therefore, if a failure does occur, the necessary parts are immediately available.

Hardware Cluster Architecture

Multiple architectures exist that address availability involving an HA hardware cluster. An HA hardware cluster consists of two or more nodes that are connected via a private, high-speed interconnect and connect to storage that is shared between all of the nodes. The storage is most likely a Storage Area Network (SAN) in a fabric configuration. Essentially, two or more servers share a common set of disks, but each server has its own memory and CPU resources. Additionally, the hardware cluster accesses a shared disk array which is also accessed by other servers.

Figure 2.1 shows an example of a basic SAN environment.

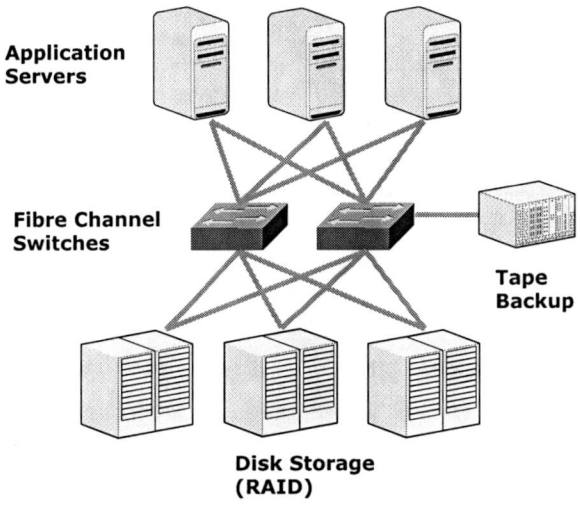

Figure 2.1   Storage Area Network

SAN environments are ideal for HA applications. They offer high levels of uptime due to the redundancy of their components. If any server fails, processing can be picked up by surviving members of the cluster. Combining multiple servers, storage devices, and network paths together with clustering software allows organizations to build a system that can recover from a failure.

NOTE The hardware architecture is merely a piece of the HA puzzle. The application software itself must also be capable of recovering from a failure while maintaining the integrity of the applications' data. It does no good for hardware to be HA if the software cannot take advantage of it. ApacheTomcat and BEA Weblogic web and application servers are examples of software that can manage and recover from a hardware system failure.

HA clusters that provide resource failover can be configured as active-passive or active-active. In an active-passive configuration, there is a primary node that runs all of the applications while the passive node does not run any of the applications (it is effectively turned off). In the event of a failure, the applications, IP addresses, and storage are failed over from the primary to the passive node and restarted. At this point the passive node is now active and is the one performing the application processing. One downside of active-passive is that one node is idle until a failure occurs. The practice of having one half of a cluster not utilized until there is a failure may be an unjustified expense.

In an active-active configuration, each node is actively serving the business applications and its users. In the event of a failure, part or all of the failed node's applications, IP addresses, and storage transition to the surviving node(s). All of the nodes in the cluster are utilized. A downside is that an imbalance of utilization across the entire cluster occurs when the remaining nodes are not able to absorb the failed node's workload. Even in the HA world, tradeoffs can impact your application and system costs, scalability and uptime.

See Figure 2.2 for an example of failover in an HA cluster running an active-passive configuration.

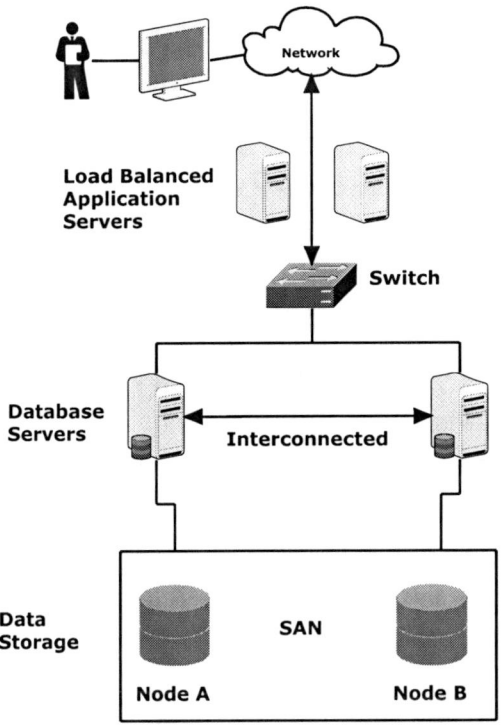

Figure 2.2   **Failover in an HA Cluster**

Figure 2.2 shows a failover in an HA cluster. Database servers located on Node A are currently installed and running, making Node A active. The databases on Node A are accessing a shared disk area on the SAN. On the passive Node B, there is database software installed and configured to access the shared disk area on the SAN, but *it is not currently running*. In the event of a failure on Node A, the database software on Node B is automatically started accessing the same database files on the SAN. Incoming requests for the application servers are routed to Node B, and the end users may not even notice the temporary failover from Node A to Node B.

In the previous architecture, we had multiple servers that could support an application, but only one node was really the primary at any given time. Under an active-active configuration, users are provided a higher level of uptime with virtually the same hardware configuration and multiple servers acting as the "primary" *at the same time*. In this configuration, there is no need to transition applications, IP addresses, and storage over to the surviving node in the event of a failure. The cluster and disk management software can be configured to allow all nodes to share the data storage concurrently and allow inter-nodal communication via the high-speed interconnect. In the case of a database server, multiple nodes can be configured to utilize the shared storage (the physical database files), communicate locking information, and pass data blocks to other nodes via the interconnect. Under this configuration, you have multiple nodes accessing the same physical database simultaneously. Of course if any one node fails, the other surviving nodes can continue processing. Additionally, because there are multiple servers doing processing for one database, the total system can handle a much heavier workload than any one server could. This is a classic example of horizontal scaling.

Storage Management

Storage management is just as critical to achieving HA as any other component. In its simplest terms, storage management is the design, administration, and care of the physical medium containing the data which the server(s) access. The storage medium could be tape or writeable compact disks; however, in this discussion, we will focus on disks

RAID (Redundant Array of Inexpensive/Independent Disks) is a method for managing individual disk storage devices to deliver low cost, high performance, and highly available data. Four important RAID levels commonly used are,

- RAID 0 – Data blocks are interleaved or striped across multiple disks. This improves performance but doesn't, by itself, improve fault tolerance or HA.

- RAID 1 – Data blocks are mirrored across multiple disks. Simply put, one disk can be mirrored to another identical disk. The idea is that by having data existing on two identical disks, downtime won't be experienced. This provides excellent fault tolerance but can be expensive to implement because it requires twice the amount of disk space you normally would need.

- RAID 5 – Data blocks are written across multiple disks in addition to parity blocks. Parity is calculated for the data and written to a parity block for the purpose of rebuilding the data in the event of a disk failure. This provides a measure of fault tolerance if a disk is lost but is not especially fast, because for every write the parity must be calculated.

- RAID 0 + 1 – A combination of RAID 0 (striping) with RAID 1 (mirroring), this level provides the best of both technologies. Data has fault tolerance without having to use a parity disk and is written across multiple disks to allow for improved performance.

Other levels of RAID do exist but these are the most commonly implemented. It is important to select the right RAID level when working towards HA.

Storage Array Networks (SANs) and Network Attached Storage (NAS) enter in to the HA discussion as they need to be configured for HA as well. Most large enterprise class systems will use a device such as a SAN, especially for large databases. Fortunately, many SAN vendors provide specialized software that provides HA features such as copying data from one SAN to another SAN which provides fault tolerance and supports disaster recovery. This facilitates the ability to host organizational systems at different physical locations, whereby data can be synchronized real-time between sites. Work with your SAN vendor to determine what specialized HA features are available for the devices you are using.

One last critical storage management item is backup and recovery. As important as an organization's data is, it is surprising how frequently system recoveries fail in time of an emergency. Normally the problem is not with the hardware or SAN itself, but in the backup and recovery procedures the administrative staff follows. It is wise to perform periodic tests to ensure that a database or system can be recovered. Detailed backup and recovery practices are covered in *Chapter 7, Disaster Recovery Planning*.

NOTE Storage solution providers like Hitachi and EMC have products that can be purchased to ease the burden of HA. These products are also used to assist with disaster recovery plans. Hitachi Data Systems has two products that allow data to be copied from one source to another. The first is Shadow Image. It provides the ability to replicate data within a storage area network (SAN) device. The other is TrueCopy, which allows data to be replicated across SANs. EMC Corporation has a product called Symmetric Remote Data Facility (SRDF) that can replicate data. It operates in one of two modes, synchronous and asynchronous. Previously, only Oracle guaranteed no data loss if implemented in the synchronous mode. This was because the order of the writes to the remote disk was not guaranteed to be in the same order under the asynchronous mode as the writes to the primary disk. Although these and other products do have restrictions and limitations, they are typically available on all models of the vendors' SAN devices.

Operating Systems

There are many different types of operating systems (OS) available, each with its own strengths and weaknesses. Most IT shops inherently have multiple OS types in their inventories. A very common model for many organizations is Microsoft Windows for the desktop or lower-end processing (e.g. email servers) with more powerful UNIX servers for more intensive processing such as database or web application servers. Mainframe systems continue to exist for large legacy systems and will likely do so for the foreseeable future. Few people would dispute that is the architecture for many organizations, but let's look at some of the factors and commonly held beliefs as to why this is the case.

- Microsoft Windows is very common on PCs or lower end servers. Reasons include that Windows is user friendly and has a very well established set of common office tools (i.e. word processors and spread sheets). Windows is the most familiar to users because of a large market share, as well as a large base of administrators available to manage these systems. Negative points against Windows are the expense, lack of user control, poor scalability when hosting a large number of users, and its reputation of sometimes being unstable. For these reasons, Windows has never had a strong history of supporting very large or mission-critical applications.

- The UNIX operation system has many vendors (i.e. Sun, HP, IBM, and many more) and maintains a strong hold on medium to large size server based systems. UNIX is very stable, scales well to support large numbers of users, gives the administrator a very high degree of control over its configuration and operation, and is supported on many different hardware platforms. Negatives are that it is designed for larger systems and not necessarily for end users' workstations, user interfaces into the system are often command line text which requires a higher skilled person to operate, and that there are a smaller number of qualified administrators than compared to Windows. However, due to its excellent stability and ability to support very large systems, UNIX remains the top choice for high-end server computing.

In recent years, the preference of operating systems has changed relatively little despite new advances in hardware, new versions of software, and the ever present marketing hype. Notable industry trends include:

- Linux operating systems are increasing in popularity. Linux is one version of a UNIX-like operating system that typically runs on smaller servers or PCs once dominated by Windows. Linux is typically inexpensive yet robust enough to turn even modestly equipped machines into viable web or database servers. It is also attempting to invade the end user workstation market with office tools to compete against Microsoft. This makes Linux very popular for small to medium sized systems.

- Microsoft Windows solutions are often more competitively priced for high demanding environments while increasing in capability to support larger systems typically once dominated by UNIX. Each release of Windows becomes better suited for larger and more complex work.

- Interest in clustering technologies and network computing architectures has increased. To take advantage of these hardware architectures, the OS often needs special software.

- Resurgence of Apple products with Mac OS has proven to be a viable operating system (which is actually based on UNIX). Supporters of Apple often have a high degree of brand loyalty.

When creating HA systems for clients with large enterprise-sized or life-critical systems, it is our experience that UNIX is still the operating system of choice for most organizations. It has the proven history, solid OS vendor support, and runs on some of the most powerful and reliable servers available. For smaller, less critical systems, UNIX is still often favored simply because it is a solid OS.

If cost is a factor and the hardware is Intel based, Linux offers many of the same benefits as UNIX but at a reduced cost. Negatives are that Linux is generally not as advanced as UNIX, and earlier versions did take some effort to get running with some advanced database tools. However, most of those problems are fixed or are being addressed. Linux is now a very common OS, especially when working with web application servers.

When working with systems that do not support large numbers of users, or depend on applications being deployed, Windows can be a viable option. For applications that need to be developed quickly, especially for relatively small to medium sized organizations, Windows often provides adequate HA service.

An organization can build a cluster of systems that have redundant servers, storage devices with multiple paths, and redundant networks. However, without the proper software to manage the overall cluster, the hardware is of little value. Equally important is that the application software needs to be able to survive and recover from a failure without corrupting data or disrupting the other nodes in the cluster. The goal is to design a system where there is no single point of failure that will bring the entire system down completely. Building HA systems is more complex than building non-HA ones. Decision makers must ensure that the organization posses the necessary expertise to build, implement, and mange an HA environment. That said, high availability systems at all appropriate tiers within the enterprise allow organizations to offer customers and users the application uptime required.

NOTE Be sure to back up all critical operating system files such as configuration files for the operating system, databases, and application components. Surprisingly enough, these important files are often forgotten.

CHAPTER 2

REFLECTION

HA systems are built on hardware and managed with software. Hardware and storage vendors have an array of solutions to increase availability. One of the best solutions is clustering. This can double the cost of hardware but provides increased performance for critical systems.

Take a few minutes to reflect on the following thoughts to help formulate ways to make your systems more highly available.

1. What hardware-related single points of failure exist in your system environment, and how can they be eliminated?

2. Do you currently have any redundant hardware or storage?

3. What operating systems are used in your organization's system environment, and why were these operating systems chosen? Are all current systems adequate?

4. Data growth will undoubtedly add to the need for increased storage, but what is the impact in terms of HA?

5. How reliable is your current hardware and storage solution? Are there any known or recurring problems that have a negative impact on availability or customer satisfaction?

6. Do you have vendor support for your hardware and storage solutions? Do you have an SLA?

7. With an understandably limited budget, which of your systems would be most beneficial to cluster in terms of hardware and storage? Can you foresee any performance benefits with a clustered solution?

Chapter 3: Databases

HA supports database environments by preserving information, interactive or not, and keeping it available at all times. No system infrastructure component is more important than the database, as the database contains critical business data. In fact, while some businesses' products are tangible objects, the products of other businesses are its data and resulting information. Hardware and software can be replaced, but data cannot – at least not without an adequate HA solution. All system components exist to support the database to some degree. Applications allow users to access and use data, hardware allows for data storage, and networks allow for data transmission. Figure 3.1 shows the importance of the database and dependencies within a typical information system architecture.

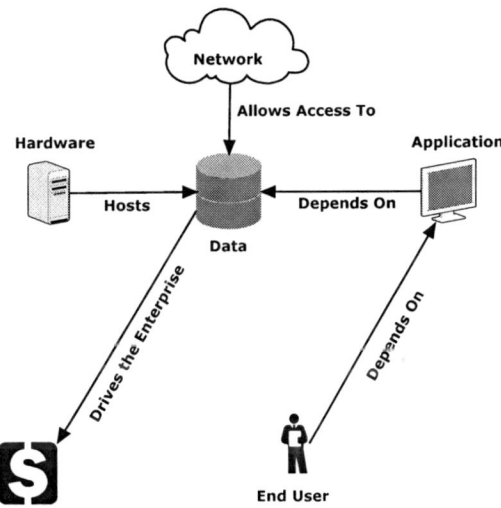

Figure 3.1   The Database in the System Infrastructure

Whereas database unavailability has often been a serious detriment to organizations, database vendors have recently begun to embrace features that support HA. Even more importantly, these new technologies have matured to a point where they can truly be trusted to provide HA. New techniques have been developed to utilize redundant system components and reduce single points of failure. This has been achieved programmatically within the database software and hardware. This chapter explores some of the best practices for ensuring HA in terms of your database environment.

Dynamics of the Database

Databases contain critical business information. Data is selected, inserted, updated, and deleted from databases, often at a rate of millions of transactions per day. Data gathered from the database is relied upon by a variety of people internal and external to the organization, including management, customers, vendors, affiliates, and end users. Table 3.1 brings light to the typical interaction that database users have with data.

Table 3.1   Database Use

Database User	How Data is Typically Used
Management	Management uses data to gather business intelligence to make responsible business decisions.
End users	End users use data to operate the organization, support internal and external customers, and conduct daily tasks critical to the life of the organization.
Customers	Customers use data to conduct business with the organization which usually has either an immediate or residual impact on revenue.
Integrated computer systems	Data in one database may automatically be supplied as an input to another separate computer system. It is not uncommon for one system to "feed" another system. For example, an inventory control system could produce automated data feeds to sales and supply chain systems. This sharing of data introduces complex dependencies between systems.

The database could possibly be the most challenging to properly configure in a true HA environment. Other system components are typically not as dynamic in nature as the database. It isn't the database itself, but rather what the database contains, the data. Power sources, computing hardware, network connections, routers, and switches are fairly static. Once in place, changes to these components are minimal compared to that of the database. Even software and application interfaces are often simpler to configure for HA than the database.

On the other hand, data is under constant renovation, or at least has the ability to change without notice. There can literally be millions of data changes in one day. This is evident just by observing the creation of database transaction log files. On a busy system, it is not uncommon to generate 100 MB of new transaction data every hour. Keeping two or more databases synchronized with changes, simultaneously without latency, is attainable but often complex and costly.

Inadequacy of Traditional Backup and Recovery

The first step in achieving HA for your database environment is with a basic database backup and recovery system. Backup and recovery is not the same as HA but is a dependency for HA. If you don't have an effective backup and recovery solution, you can forget having an HA system. Despite its importance, it is amazing how many organizations do not have an adequate backup and recovery plan or proven implementation. Many organizations do not properly backup data or backup frequently enough. Some organizations have been "backing up" data for years only to discover in a time of failure that the backups taken are not sufficient.

Even more IT departments have some sort of a backup and recovery plan but no documentation. Nor have they ever tested a recovery. From our experience, it's not "if" a failure will occur but "when." With so many dependencies in a typical IT environment, your database is almost guaranteed to crash or become corrupted at some point. A power failure, a bad hard drive, user error, software bug, program error, and virus are just a few threats to the availability, security, and continuity of your database.

There are two basic types of database backups that can be taken: the cold backup and the hot backup. Cold backups are sometimes referred to as "offline" backups, while hot backups are often referred to as "online" backups. Table 3.2 describes the basic principles of each backup method.

Table 3.2   Backup Principles

Method	Description
Cold/ offline backup	**Performing a Cold Backup** • Shutdown database, copy database files to backup tape or disk, restart database. *During this time the database is unavailable to users because it is shutdown.* • Backup and recovery time is lengthy, as a database snapshot is taken with each backup. • Can only recover to last backup, so all transactions are lost between last backup and time of failure. **When to Use a Cold Backup** • As an offline backup, it is appropriate for databases that are static, meaning data is infrequently added or updated. • Adequate for data warehouses and other databases that are query only. Since the database is shutdown during backups, this method alone is not conducive to HA systems.
Hot/ online backup	**Performing a Hot Backup** • Database files are backed up to tape or disk while database is running. *During this time the database is available.* • Special internal database controls allow copying of relevant data files/software while data is being changed. • Slight performance impact during hot backups, but *the database is available for normal processing.* **When to Use a Hot Backup** • Appropriate for dynamic databases and databases that have small windows for backups and maintenance. • Most databases are backed up via hot backup. Recovering a database from a hot backup recovers the database to a specific point in time. Supports recovery up to the time of failure with minimal or no data loss. • Since the database is available during backups, hot or online database backups play a critical role in HA systems.

Some form of a backup is usually required to guarantee adequate recoverability for critical databases. Often a mix of weekly or monthly cold backups with nightly hot backups provides a satisfactory level of backups. Given a valid database backup and all transaction logs since the backup, most database administrators can recover a database to any given point in time since the last backup.

Keeping copies of database transaction logs is as critical as the database backup itself. What happens is that as data changes (e.g. a customer buys a product), a log of that data change is written to a file outside the database. These transaction logs record everything that has occurred inside that database. In a recovery situation, the administrator restores the most recent backup of the database. He then automatically applies transaction logs generated since that backup to reapply database changes. Once complete, the database is "current" with all changes that have been made to it prior to the failure (i.e. no data has been lost). Additionally, the administrator can stop the recovery at any given point in time to effectively reset the database to a time prior to the crash. The key factors here are having a recent backup (to reduce the number of transaction logs to apply or "replay") and having copies of the transaction logs available.

Major database software vendors handle logging methods that record database changes as they commit completed transactions to the database. In the event of a failure, the data can be rolled back to a consistent point in time without corruption. Several operating systems have also adopted the ability to roll back transactions. Most database vendors and many third party companies provide administrative software to manage these database backups and simplify their recovery. It is important for the technical staff to be proficient in backup and recovery tools used for their specific database.

Historically, database "HA" was addressed with standard backup and recovery method. If the database had a major failure, administrators recovered from tape or disk and then recovered the database to a point in time prior to the failure. This practice was capable of handling recovery, but database processing and user access was on hold until it was complete. For large databases, this took a significant amount of time, equating to lost revenue or poor customer service. In that respect, we see how backup and recovery is not the same as true HA.

Figure 3.2 shows how inadequate the traditional backup and recovery method is compared to a high availability solution. The objectives of a high availability solution are to reduce the risk of database failure and minimize or even eliminate downtime due to failure. A backup and recovery solution alone only intends to guarantee recoverability. While recoverability is necessary, unavailability of the database during the recovery process (which could take hours or even days for very large databases) could be so severe that it is just as bad as not being able to recover the database.

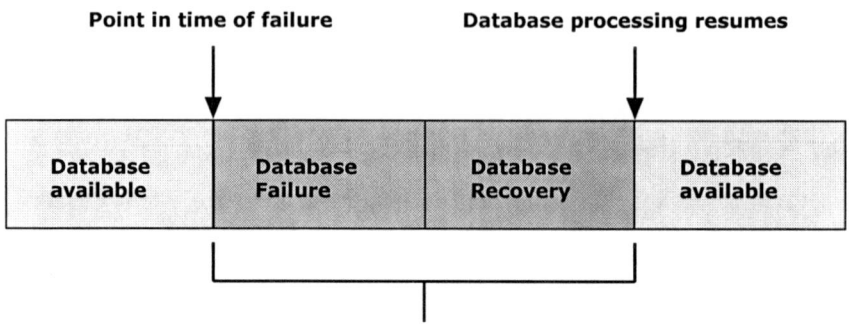

Figure 3.2   Traditional Backup and Recovery Inadequacy

NOTE Traditional backup and recovery only provides recoverability, not high availability. However, having a solid backup and recovery plan in place takes priority over implementing high availability. Although this seems obvious, it is horrifying how many organizations we have encountered that do not adequately backup their data. Even those that think their systems are recoverable often learn the opposite and encounter an even bigger challenge with a lack of documentation.

While traditional backup and recovery is a necessary ingredient to the HA recipe, it is still not true HA unless the hardware and software single points of failure are identified and eliminated. It is critical to implement the system with fault tolerance and automatic transparent failover so that if one or more individual failures occur, the database is still fully available to the users with no noticeable downtime. The rest of this chapter addresses acceptable and common options for making your database highly available.

Secondary Database Environments

An excellent solution for database HA is to have a secondary database environment. Another common term for a secondary environment is a standby database – a term used by Oracle Corporation. The basic concept is that you have a copy of the production database that is constantly being updated but unavailable to users for access. The standby database exists in case the main production database fails and becomes unavailable. In such a case, all appropriate users and applications are directed to the standby database. This acts as a failover solution, so when the primary site fails or is destroyed, users will automatically begin using the secondary site. *This does not necessarily enhance the durability of the primary site but provides a fault-tolerant alternative site in the event of a failure at the primary site.*

NOTE   In a standby, or secondary database environment, a failover occurs when the secondary database is activated after the primary database has failed. The failover process can be either manual or automatic depending on how set up.

Figure 3.3 shows a basic standby database environment.

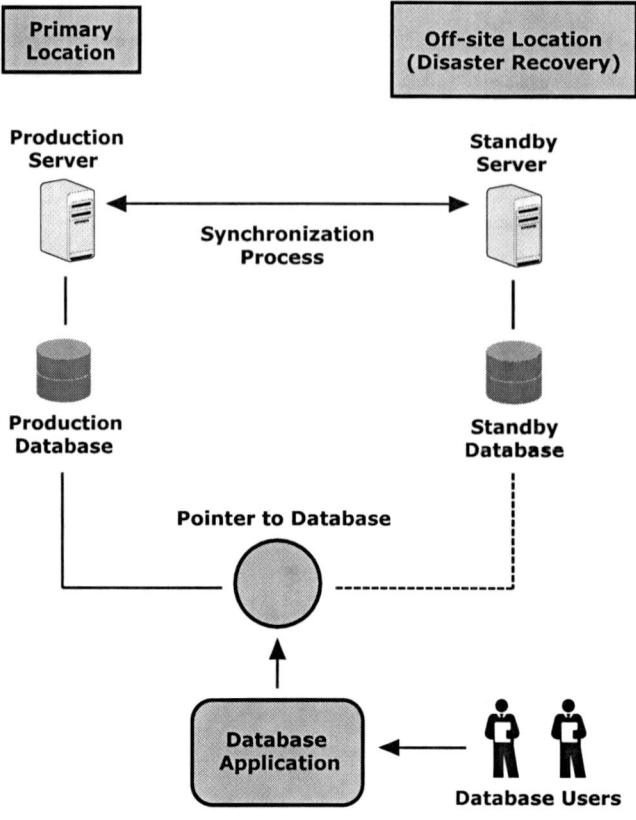

Figure 3.3   Standby Database

The challenge with a secondary database environment is keeping it in sync with the production database environment. There must be a procedure, preferably automated, to ensure both environments are in sync at all times. This is typically done by shipping database transaction logs from the primary site to the secondary site where they are automatically applied. This means that any transaction or change made to the primary also occurs at the secondary. Oracle Corporation's product, Dataguard, provides a graphical interface and automated process for managing your standby database environment. Third party vendors also have products that provide similar functionality.

Figure 3.4 illustrates Dataguard's role in standby database management.

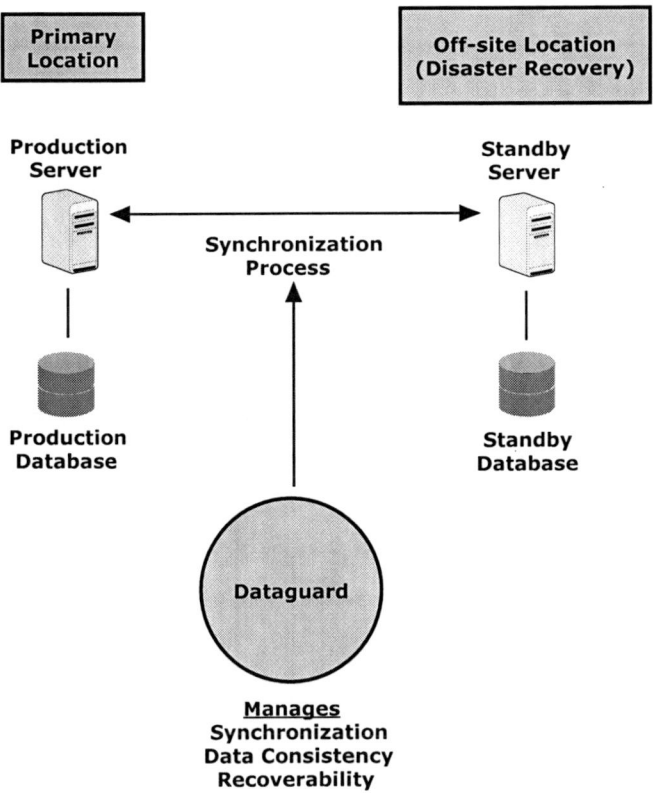

Figure 3.4   Oracle Corporation's Dataguard

In the event of a total failure with the primary site, the secondary site is turned "on," and users begin accessing that database instead. The switchover to the second site can occur in minutes, and depending on the overall system architecture, the user may never even notice the switchover. Because the secondary site was continually updated with transaction logs of the primary site, there is little or no data loss associated with the switchover. While users are accessing the secondary site, the primary site can be rebuilt or recovered without incurring downtime. Once the primary site is recovered and synchronized with the secondary site, a second switchover can occur to move back to the original primary site.

NOTE It is sometimes not enough just to recover a database in the event of a failure. An outage or disaster may occur that impacts the application, network, or the web application servers. Looking beyond just the database and considering system recovery as a whole is important when planning HA.

It is possible to implement the secondary database environment over a Wide Area Network (WAN) to a remote site, benefiting both the HA plan and Disaster Recovery Plan (DRP). This is covered in greater detail in *Chapter 7, Disaster Recovery Planning*. The following case study explains how a standby database could have helped one system at a critical time.

CASE STUDY

Financial Services Firm

Legally obligated to provide critical reports every fiscal quarter, accountants work around the clock, seven days a week, during the first two weeks of the quarter to meet this deadline. As a high-profile financial services firm, failure to meet the regulatory deadline would result in severe ramifications.

Problem:

Two days before finishing a quarterly cycle, the one and only database server crashed and could not be restarted. A myriad of multiple hardware failures combined with amateur mistakes by the recovery staff shut down production of the reports. The applications on that database server were completely unusable for four days before finally recovering the server.

Lessons learned:

The cost of system administrators and vendor-support staff working around-the-clock shifts was the least concern of the financial firm. Legal fines totaled over $250,000, client satisfaction was temporarily affected, and market share decreased a little over one percent.

Simply having an HA solution in place would have prevented this costly situation. Investing in a backup database and properly training staff on backup and recovery procedures would have saved this company from financial and legal penalties.

Clustered Database Environments

The best scenario to support database HA is to have multiple database servers running that access a single set of data. This provides both fault tolerance in the event of a single database failure as well as horizontal scaling to improve performance and system throughput (e.g. more servers processing incoming user requests). Oracle Corporation allows this to be done with Real Application Clusters (RAC), and IBM Corporation does this with partitioning. IBM's partitioning is not table and data partitioning. You can also partition data, but for purposes of this book, partitioning with DB2/UDB is having multiple servers accessing the same set of data. In this book, we'll use the term clustering or database server clustering to be generic.

NOTE Horizontal scaling is accomplished by spreading processing across multiple resources. A clustered database environment can involve redundancy across network, system, database, and application components. Horizontal scaling not only supports high availability, but can be used to boost performance dramatically.

Figure 3.5 illustrates the concept of clustering. As you can see, multiple database instances that reside on multiple physical servers can be configured to access a single data source. Typically, the data source resides in a SAN (storage area network) or RAID (Redundant Array of Independent Disks) configuration, ensuring data redundancy if a failure occurs on the storage side. If database server 2 fails, users can access servers 1, 3, and 4 to access the data without interruption. If Data 1 fails in the storage area network, the same data can be found on Data 2. For a more detailed discussion of storage management, see *Chapter 2, Hardware, Storage, and Operating Systems*. Again, it is important to note that clustering doesn't necessary reduce the frequency of failures but hides their impact to the user community by providing fault tolerance.

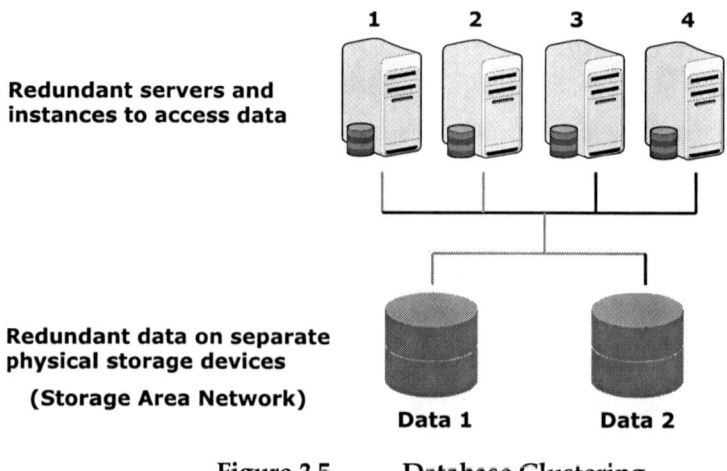

Figure 3.5   Database Clustering

Redundant data should be maintained for optimal protection (e.g. via the appropriate level of RAID) for the disk drives. Some vendors also enable data redundancy within the database configuration. For example, Oracle allows specifying either simple or complex data redundancy when using Automatic Storage Management (ASM) to control data storage. A key advantage to setting up ASM is that disks configured at the OS level with redundancy provide dual redundancy. This is an improvement but also takes more disk space to configure and maintain which is necessary if either RAID 5 or mirroring is implemented. Under a configuration such as RAID 5, it is important to consider the probability of losing two drives containing the same data (for a mirrored implementation), or simultaneously losing a drive and the parity drive before you get the first failed drive replaced and synched up with data. Disk drives are always a single point of failure, but you can introduce redundancy with RAID to minimize the negative impact for when they do fail.

Some of the advantages a clustered database environment holds over a secondary database environment include better horizontal scalability for data growth and higher performance for heavy-hit database applications. If the system load increases (e.g. more users are accessing the system), you can add a new cluster member rather than adding more memory or CPUs to the existing servers. Unlike the secondary database environment, the clustered environment is a server room solution where all machines are located in one geographic location. This addresses HA concerns for routine failures but does not address site specific disasters. However, with a clustered database also in a standby configuration, you can combine the concepts of secondary and clustered environments to maximize scalability, performance, recoverability, and availability. This configuration would provide the best of both worlds in terms of clusters and standby systems but comes at a financial expense to purchase the hardware, licensing, support. Technical expenses also exist in terms of increased complexity and maintenance.

Managing Memory Synchronization

Whether your HA environment consists of a secondary database environment or a clustered database solution, memory synchronization may pose a problem. These days, databases do not process data directly from disk; the data is staged in memory for better performance. In most hardware architectures, memory isn't shared across servers. Somehow data changes in memory need to be kept in synch, or you have to force writes to disk and then read back from disk to ensure the most current data. This can cause performance issues, because now you've reduced the efficiency of storing recently accessed data in memory. This depends on how the clustering of the server has been implemented for a given application. Oracle requires an interconnect between the clustered servers to allow data to be more efficiently synched while still in memory.

NOTE Managing memory synchronization becomes more important in a clustered database environment, especially as memory becomes more affordable and applications are created to optimize memory usage. Fortunately, vendors are providing more sophisticated software with improved memory management capabilities.

Figure 3.6 shows the possible synchronization issue that may exist in a clustered database environment.

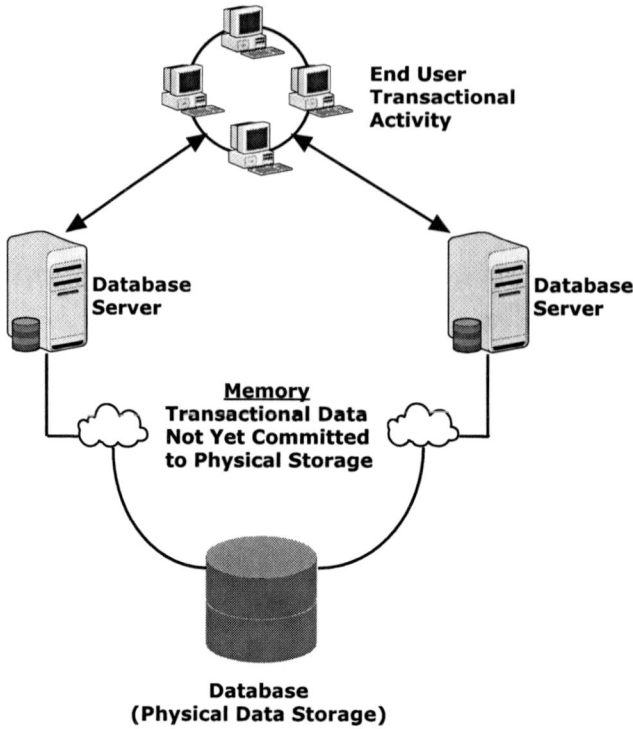

Figure 3.6   Synchronization of Memory

NOTE The interconnect between the databases is not the only level of added complexity. There is an interconnect between the servers and corresponding software which must be managed by the system administration staff. This additional level of hardware and software adds complexity to the system and increases the possibility of bugs. Ensure your technical staff is proficient with their clustering software and tools to reduce the possibility of human error.

Another option is to have multiple applications or subsets of transactions from one large application split. This ensures they will either not compete for the same data nor have the updates of shared data performed by one server. This dramatically reduces the overhead of keeping data in memory synched up. Of course, if a server were to fail, transactions would then be executed from one of the other servers and there would be no performance impact unless there is just too much work for the remaining server(s) to handle.

Yet another option is to have servers clustered just for failover purposes. In this manner, all users and batch jobs would be run against the primary server. If the primary server were to fail, the database on the secondary server would automatically be started and users would be routed to the secondary server with little or no downtime. Depending on how the application is written, users may need to reconnect to the application and repeat their last transaction or command; a minor inconvenience compared to a total loss of service. This solution still requires a cluster configuration but is conceptually simpler to implement and manage than a cluster where the databases on both servers are running simultaneously. Given that many database cluster implementations require special and expensive licensing, clustered servers can also reduce those costs.

NOTE   A very common clustered database configuration involves Oracle Real Application Clusters (RAC). This software interacts with the underlying cluster configuration to manage and allow simultaneous access to a single database via multiple nodes. In the event of a node failure, the database manages the cleanup process of that node while still servicing requests from surviving nodes. This is essentially the same database as single nodes but with additional features that allow it to work in a multi-node clustered environment. A RAC configuration consists of multiple Oracle instances running on multiple nodes. These instances share a single physical database. Instances communicate via a cluster interconnect. Instances can leave and join the cluster dynamically. Each instance serves user transactions independently using the common database.

Figure 3.7 shows an example of a clustered database environment. The figure shows two databases that support accounts payable and receivable (A/P and A/R) for a typical organization. A switch manages user application requests to interconnected database servers, which in turn possess independent connections to a shared data source.

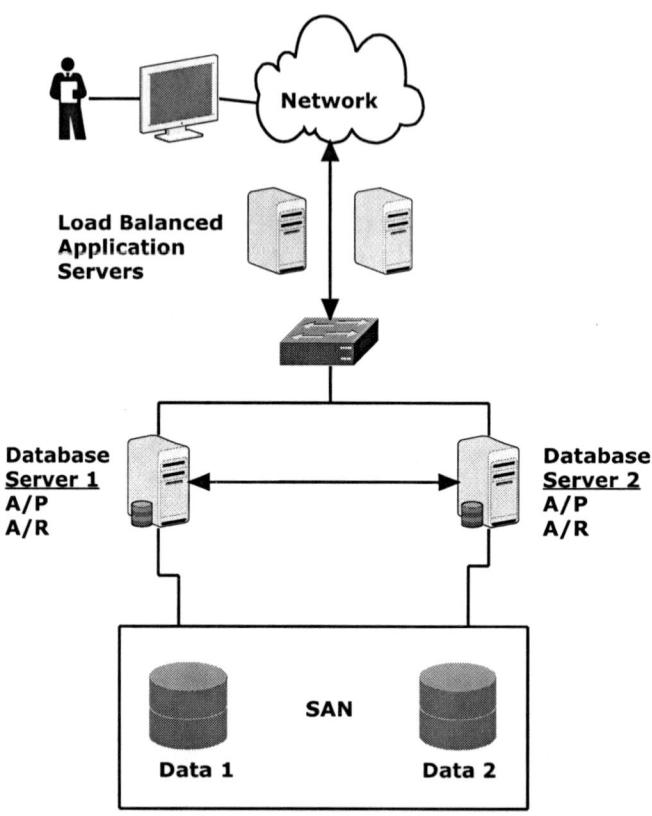

Figure 3.7   Clustered Database Environment

Referring back to Figure 3.7, note that database servers 1 and 2 are each running independent database instances, but each instance is accessing the same physical database files in the SAN. The instances on database servers 1 and 2 are aware of each other and communicate necessary synchronization information between each other. Both servers are in an active configuration and performing real work and; neither is in a passive standby mode. This allows for maximum processing throughput for the system. If either node fails, processing will still continue on the surviving node. As the workload requirements for the application increase, additional nodes may be added.

Database applications can be written in many different manners. To fully implement transparent application failover, the application must be written in a manner so that a user's session information is retained and shared across application servers. This further protects the user's sessions if the database server being routed to fails, and transactions have to be rerouted to a secondary server. This configuration is the most complex as it is dependent on the application being coded correctly, the web application server tier being clustered, and the database servers being clustered as well. However, with modern HA technology, an implementation such as this is possible assuming the necessary system architecture engineering has occurred. In Figure 3.8 we see how one such implementation might look.

Figure 3.8 shows redundancy implemented at every system level. Users access a cluster of redundant web application servers that interact with a cluster of databases pulling data from a redundant SAN, all with redundant network infrastructure and load balancing. An identical standby system has been established at a remote site in the event the primary site experiences a major failure. Transaction logs are automatically shipped from the primary to the secondary site where they are continually applied to the database, so both database systems are in synch. Switching to the standby site is relatively simple, and users may not even notice that it has occurred.

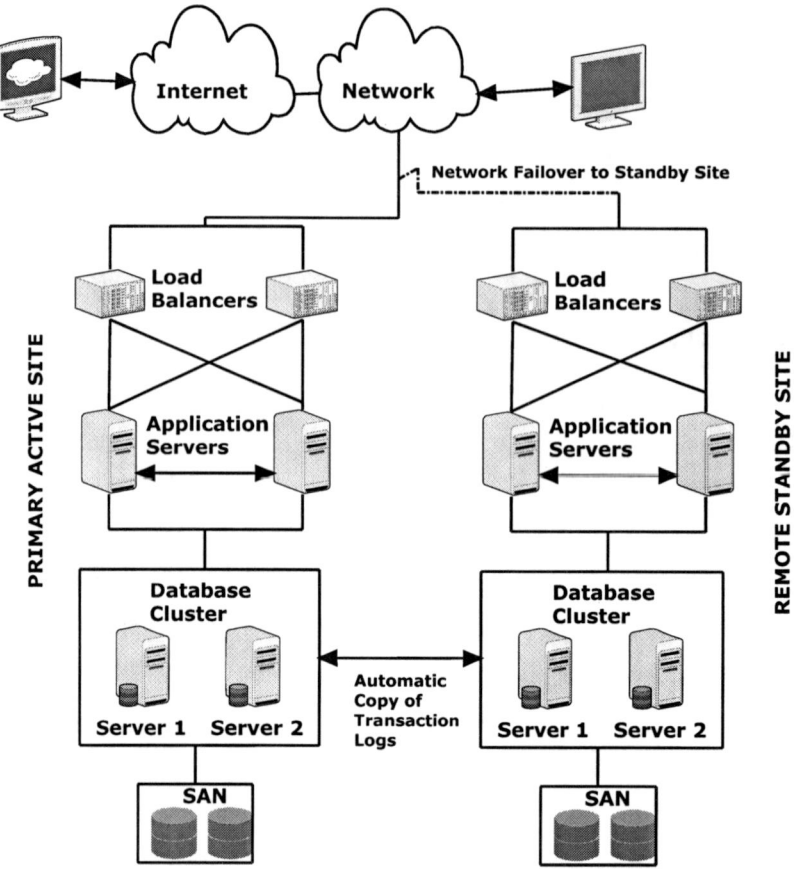

Figure 3.8   Potential HA Database Solution

Such an implementation, as shown in Figure 3.8, is not for the faint of heart, as the implementation is complex and expensive (but well worth it for many organizations). A fully implemented HA solution's system diagram will look very similar to this one.

The remainder of this book explores HA options for other system components that interact with the database, starting with *Chapter 4, Web and Application Servers*.

**CHAPTER 3
REFLECTION**

Ultimately, data is the core of any system. All system components exist to support and process data. In this chapter, two important approaches to improving database availability were discussed: secondary database environments and database clustering. A secondary is a cost-effective solution that provides HA for many database environments. However, a clustered database environment provides strong HA capability and supports more concurrent processing.

Take a few minutes to reflect on the following thoughts to help formulate ways to make your systems more highly available.

1. How critical is your data to daily operations?

2. When must your data be available to users (SLA requirement)?

3. How is your data growing or transforming, and will the future of your organization be affected by its evolution?

4. Do you have confidence in your backup and recovery procedure? Has a recovery ever been successfully achieved or at least tested? Is your backup and recovery procedure documented and updated as your business and system needs change?

5. If your database crashed right now, how much data would be lost? What would be the cost to your organization?

6. How old is your database software? Is it supported by the database vendor? Do you get support from a third party vendor?

7. What applications are integrated with your database? What single points of failure are recognized due to this integration?

8. For your most critical database, would you go with a secondary or clustered database environment?

CHAPTER 4: WEB AND APPLICATION SERVERS

The previous chapter provided an overview of how databases can be engineered to provide high availability. This chapter looks at the architecture of web and application interfaces as they relate to high availability. Before discussing application availability, let's first examine the components that support the web and application servers. These components must also provide high availability.

Role of the Web Server

High availability of the web server is a priority. Web servers are listeners for incoming requests from the Internet. They display information (web pages), initiate processing, and/or access an online program. The role of the traditional web server is somewhat limited to merely receiving incoming requests, displaying graphical content (text, documents, images, sound), and processing relatively simple requests (online forms).

This type of server is useful for supporting relatively simple websites that display a company's name, product list, contact and address information, or allow a user to sign up for a mailing list or post simple questions. Examples of typical web server implementations include:

- Displaying HTML pages in response to requests from a user's PC (for example, hosting HTML pages for a simple website)

- Providing files for download such as informational Adobe PDF files, Microsoft Word documents, or simple text files

- Displaying image files, pictures, or sound and movie content

- Managing web links to other websites

- Having simple online forms where people accessing a website can enter their name and email address to receive more information

- Posting a simple question to the website

- Encrypting data as it is transmitted between the web server and the user's PC using SSL (Secure Sockets Layer)

Some websites appear flashy with graphics and sound but are still primarily used for the visual presentation of information. Specifically, they display information well but do not do much in the processing of that information. More complex processing is performed by the application server as we will see in the next section. Despite its processing limitations, the web server is useful as a gateway to complex web applications and portals.

Role of the Application Server

Web servers do little more than serve static information in response to requests. For more intensive processing, the application server does the real work. Application servers work behind the web server to process information entered into a web server and then return the results back to the web server for presentation to the user. For example, consider a customer who wants to order a product from a website. The customer would enter his name and address information in to an online form on a web server. He would also enter what product he wants to buy, the quantity, and his credit card information. It is the application server that takes that information from the web server, saves it into a database showing a new product order, sends the credit card information to the credit card company to make the sale, generates the product shipping request to the shipping company, and finally updates the appropriate product inventory information. The application server does all this behind the scenes and then routes the order confirmation number back to the web server for display to the customer's browser.

How Web and Application Servers Work Together

In reality, what most people refer to as web servers are combination web application servers. When combined into a single product, web servers and application servers provide the functionality of both listening for incoming requests and displaying content while processing those requests in a meaningful way. Generally speaking, most web server products exist as a web server with integrated application server components.

The most common web server is Apache. It is fast, reliable, flexible, and free. It also easily integrates with multitudes of other web products including application servers. Depending on the type of processing required and the programming languages chosen, different types of application servers are integrated with the web server. This allows system architects to mix and match the best web server and application server products together depending on their specific needs. Larger software vendors integrate preexisting web and application server products in to product suites, allowing them to sell a more feature-rich product. For example, many database companies have released web application server products that are already configured to integrate in to its databases. This allows a company already heavily vested in a specific company's database product to use that same company's web product with the promise of better integration, performance, and overall support.

Regardless of the origin of the web application server, each component still performs the same essential functions as previously described. In Figure 4.1, we see the relationship between web and application server.

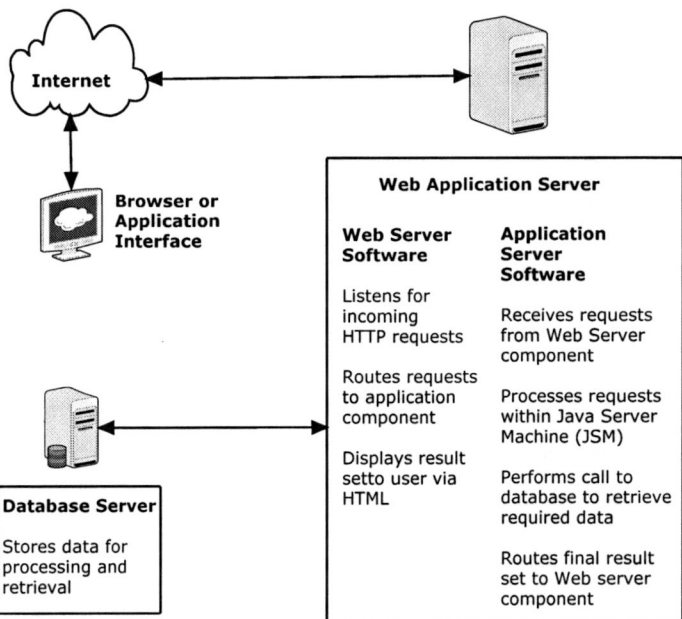

Figure 4.1   **Web Application Server Integration**

Figure 4.1 shows that the web server software is responsible for receiving the requests for the user's web browser. It then passes that information to the web application software also hosted on the same physical server. In this example, a Java application and the processing occur within a Java Virtual Machine (JVM). During the processing, it is necessary to access a database located on a different server. After the data is retrieved from the database and the results are processed with the application software, they are neatly formatted by the web server for user display.

Redundant Web Application Servers

Running an online application or website with only one web application server is conceptually and technically simple but does not give us high availability in the event of failure. This standalone configuration is common in many systems but it is subject to failures such as the following:

- Web server software or physical server crashes

- Application server software or physical server crashes

- High level of simultaneous requests flooding and overloading the web server, rendering it unable to respond (denial of a service attack)

- Poorly-written code or a long-running process in the application server renders it unable to respond to new requests

- Routine maintenance or upgrade of the web or application server takes it offline so it is unable to service requests

To guard against these threats, it is advisable to have redundant web and application server components. This redundancy is crucial to highly available web applications.

As with any other system component, adding redundancy to web components does *not* decrease the number of actual failures. In fact, the more web application servers you have, the greater the odds of a component failure. This redundancy provides inherent fault tolerance. A system is fault tolerant when it continues to work, even at a reduced capacity, despite suffering failures in one or more components. When designing HA systems, implementing fault tolerance is one of the most critical factors.

Figure 4.2 shows how fault tolerance is achieved with a system of redundant web application servers.

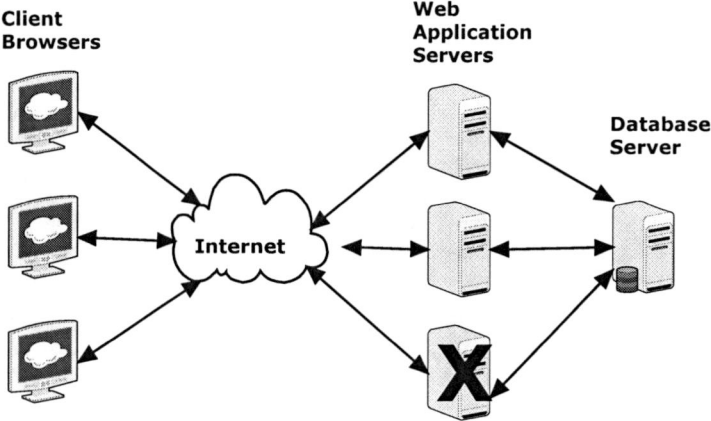

* Server crashed and is no longer available. Processing still continues across surviving two servers.

Figure 4.2   Redundant Web Application Servers

Figure 4.2 displays three separate web application servers implemented in a redundant configuration. Incoming requests from the network come into any one of the three web application servers for processing. If any one or two of the web application servers fails, incoming requests are still processed by surviving servers. In the example above, one server is down, but processing still occurs on the other two servers.

Fault-tolerant systems are easily scalable. As system demand increases, additional web application servers can be added to increase total processing power. This type of expansion is known as horizontal scaling.

In contrast, increasing processing capability by adding more CPU and memory resources to existing servers is referred to as vertical scaling. It is easier to scale vertically, as it doesn't require network reconfiguration.

However, vertical scaling does not inherently provide the fault tolerance necessary for HA systems. Furthermore, vertical scaling is limited by hardware constraints. When dealing with web application servers, it is best to scale horizontally.

NOTE Fault-tolerant systems are easily scalable. This is especially important in a web computing environment. In such an environment, it is often difficult to predict the number of concurrent users and amount of activity. Web application servers need to be configured with scalability in mind from inception. An increase in system activity, which often connotes an increase in revenue, should not have a negative impact on performance and customer satisfaction.

Clustered Web Application Servers

There are two types of clustering technology: hardware and software. With hardware clustering, two or more physical servers share hardware resources such as common disk area. With software clustering, there is no physical dependence or link between individual servers. The clustering occurs between software components installed on each server. Hardware clustering is more common with database servers while software clustering is more common on application servers.

In the world of web application servers, a cluster is two or more identically configured web application servers supporting one or more websites or applications. Each member of the cluster can process an entire incoming request or transaction independently. However, each member recognizes that it is part of a team and works as such. Each member continually checks the status of every other cluster member to determine if anyone is busy, has failed, or otherwise is not able to process requests. If any one web or application server component is busy, other cluster members take on extra requests until that one member is no longer busy. If a component has failed, other cluster members automatically try to restart it. When a member drops off the network (i.e. a server reboot), other members recognize this and stop routing additional requests to that member until it has rejoined the network and cluster. Finally, the status of each process application state is replicated across the cluster. If a member dies in the middle of a process, other members can automatically resume that transaction to successful completion without the user even knowing of the failure. This action is referred to as failover and it is critical if the web user needs to be able to work uninterrupted despite what problems may happen on the web infrastructure. Figure 4.3 shows how a redundant system has been converted in to a cluster, taking advantage of load balancing and cluster intercommunication.

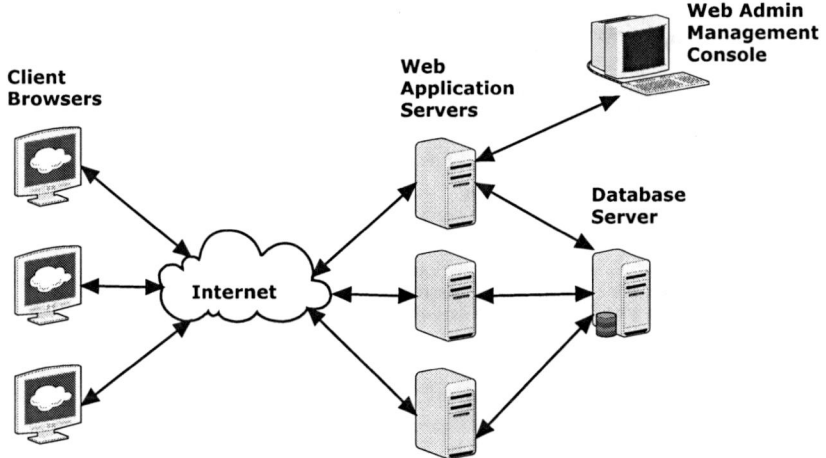

* Up/down status and application process status replicated across each cluster member. Workload is evenly distributed between each member automatically.

Figure 4.3   Web Application Server Cluster

Each self-contained web application server is a member of the cluster and can process requests individually. However, each member also communicates with every other member checking up/down status, routing requests between each other, and in the event of a failure, picking up current requests so they are not lost (and are transparent to the user). The web administrator can manage all three web application servers from one central location.

Most types of web application servers support the clustering shown in Figure 4.3. However, many servers also support an even greater degree of segmentation and clustering between web application server components. Many products allow separation (physical or logical) of the web versus the application server components and allow clustering between each component. This permits an even greater degree of fault tolerance and load balancing between components as shown in Figure 4.4.

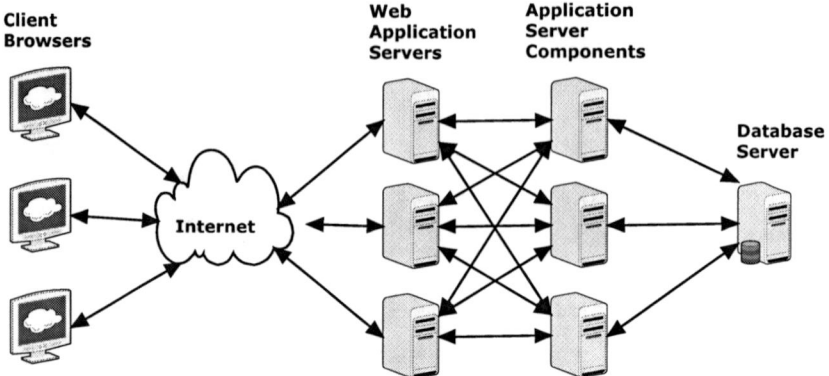

* Any component in the cluster may share processing load with any other component. All members in the cluster share up/down status and replicate application process state.

Figure 4.4   **Advanced Web Application Clustering**

In Figure 4.4, each component is logically separated within the cluster. Each member of the cluster is aware of the existence and processing status of every other component in the cluster. Advanced load-balancing algorithms ensure that work is evenly disturbed between each component to promote maximum performance. Additionally, fault tolerance, death detection with automatic restart, failover, and recovery of failed transactions exist with this configuration at a more granular level.

When working with web application servers, clustering is a beneficial technology but has a few drawbacks. Clustering is generally more difficult to set up for the web administrator, but the difficulty level varies depending on the software. Some overhead exists because of constant cross communication between each cluster component. Additional background processes exist that manage these cluster members and add complexity. Despite these drawbacks, clustering technology is sometimes the best way to enhance HA with web systems.

Network Load Balancing Options

The previous examples showed the Internet as an Internet Network cloud where incoming requests were entered and then evenly distributed between each web server. While that is the job of a properly configured network, it is an oversimplification. It is recommended to provide a degree of redundancy in a network device so if any component fails, communications continue. When working with web application servers, the load balancer is a key network device.

Load balancers are network devices that take incoming network requests and route them to one or more web servers for processing. They determine which set of web servers receive a new incoming request based on a load-balancing algorithm. They ensure that incoming web requests are distributed evenly over the pool of available web servers waiting for requests. The load balancer uses various algorithms such as round robin, least recently used, most heavily used, random, and weighted average to distribute requests so that no one web server is overloaded. Load balancers can be configured so that subsequent network requests from a specific client browser are directed to the same web server in an attempt to maintain session state.

Figure 4.5 shows how a load balancer may be deployed.

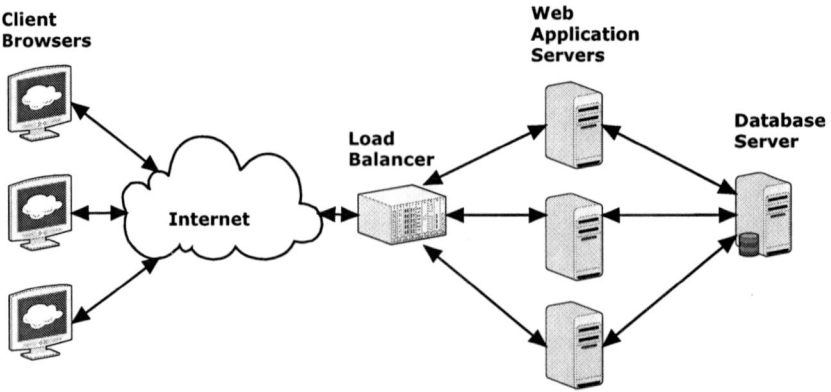

Figure 4.5   Load Balancing Devices

Figure 4.5 displays a network load balancer located in front of three web servers. The load balancer receives the incoming web request and determines which of the three web servers is least busy and most capable to accept the web request. The initial request from that browser is then routed to a particular web server, and then future communication from that same browser can be routed to the same web server.

Load balancers can exist as standalone network devices or they can, and ideally should, be clustered or deployed redundantly. They can also exist as either software components installed on a normal server (including a web server) or be purchased as dedicated hardware devices. Some load balancer products also include tools known as caching servers.

A caching server is a device that stores graphical web content such as HTML pages, documents, images, or even fragments of documents so they can be quickly provided in response to incoming web requests, so the web server does not need to provide them. The idea is to store frequently accessed content in a memory cache in front of the web server so that the web server does not spend time and resources parsing the request and displaying the same piece of content over and over. This provides a performance boost for users while reducing the workload on web servers.

For example, imagine the front page for a busy website. Every user accessing that site sees the same HTML blocks and images. Instead of making a web server generate the same presentation thousands of times, it generates that page once initially, stores it on the caching server, and then the caching server represents that page to each user requesting it. If the request is unique or the content is not in the cache area, then the request is routed to the web server for normal processing. The caching rules for what can and cannot be cached can become elaborate but are sometimes worth exploring for busy websites. And of course, caching servers can and should be clustered or deployed redundantly.

Complete HA Implementation

There is more to supporting web application servers than just setting up a website. First we saw that because web servers and application servers are fundamentally different, they can be separated and implemented in redundant manner. Then we saw how they can be clustered to provide more intelligent processing and failover than independent servers. We also examined the role of load balancers and caching servers.

Setting up a full HA web environment can be difficult. To help identify all the pieces needed, we see in Figure 4.6 a system with all the components we have discussed.

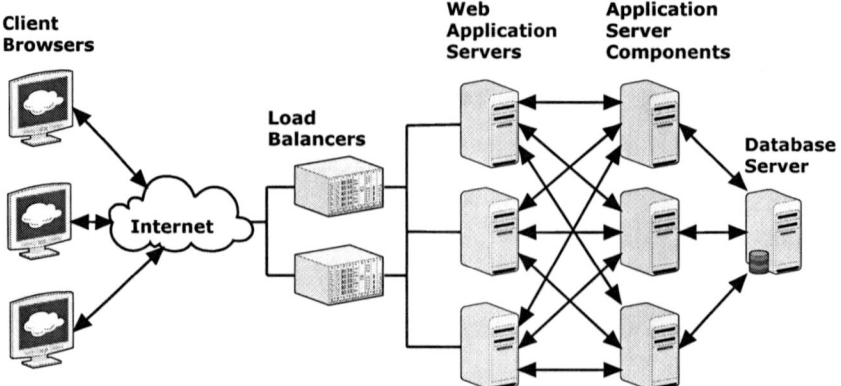

Figure 4.6   **Full HA Implementation**

Figure 4.6 displays deployed redundant components. From the time the incoming request hits the load balancers through the web application server cluster and to the clustered databases, we have redundancy providing us fault tolerance and the ability to sustain large numbers of simultaneous requests. Implementations such as this are what is needed to support large or mission-critical websites and web applications.

CHAPTER 4
REFLECTION

As the Internet and web resources have become acceptable methods by which organizations communicate, web computing has become a critical ingredient to the system environment. Web and application interfaces allow worldwide users to get the data they need, and if an interface is unavailable or appears to be unavailable for any reason, the perception to the user is that the "system" is down. To a system user or customer, perception is reality, and both misperception and actual system unavailability have a negative impact on the bottom line.

Take a few minutes to reflect on the following thoughts to help formulate ways to make your systems more highly available.

1. Do you currently have any web components to your system? If so, how critical are these components to revenue, customer satisfaction, and daily operations?

2. If you don't currently have any web components, how might the Internet itself threaten security and availability?

3. How important is it for your applications to be scalable? Consider scalability when thinking about HA.

4. As your data, customer base, and system-user base all grow, what impact do you foresee on your applications? How will performance be affected? Will increased requests for data result in decreased performance? If so, how will you handle decreased performance's affect on availability? What steps are you taking now to plan for growth?

5. What is your organization's plan, if any, to begin deploying more of your critical applications to the web computing platform? What benefits might your organization and customers experience via web computing?

Chapter 5: Networking

The previous chapters discussed how to make servers, applications, and databases robust and highly available. Those concepts are very important, but without the network infrastructure directing traffic behind the scenes, an important part of your high availability design is missing. This chapter looks at what it takes to build a reliable and secure HA network.

Highly Available Networks

High availability to your network is very subjective. HA requirements depend on your industry, business needs, and how available the environment must be. Is the amount of acceptable downtime in minutes, hours, or days? Minutes per year sounds attractive but entails huge cost tradeoffs. If your organization requires that level of availability, redundancy should be provided so that maintenance can be performed on any given portion of your network without downtime. This chapter explores the concepts and best practices of network infrastructure design. Additionally, it takes a closer look at how each component works together to provide confidentiality, integrity, and availability for your network.

Network HA Concepts

Building a highly available network involves more than just installing a pair of routers or switches and plugging everything in. Unfortunately, that is what frequently happens. Two other concepts are integral to HA. The first is confidentiality. It is important to remember that the network is the core of an entire IT operation. Maintaining confidentiality is important, because without proper segmentation, segregation, and access control, anyone can potentially access network data. It is common to think of access control and confidentiality controls being handled at the server or application level. While that is not entirely wrong, it is not entirely correct either. The security and availability of an environment should be approached in layers. Build robustness from both a network level and application level. If one fails or is breached, other layers of protection and redundancy remain. A lapse in confidentiality opens the door for data theft, malicious attacks, or data tampering that can lead to reduced availability.

Integrity would be the next important aspect to consider. If an infrastructure insuring the integrity of your data is not provided, then corrupt or compromised data could result. Integrity can be insured through many methods, but this chapter focuses on ones that can be implemented on the network. This includes network intrusion detection and prevention, Network Admission Control (NAC), logging, access to network devices, and verification of configurations.

When you put these concepts together with the proper mix of hardware and a well-trained staff, you have the ingredients for a highly available network. The following are the main components to consider when improving the availability of your infrastructure.

- Internet connectivity
- Routing and switching
- Firewalls and security
- DNS infrastructure
- Network management

Internet Connectivity

One of the most important components to concentrate on is Internet connectivity. The Internet is the hardest component to control; therefore, it is critical to design as much redundancy and robustness as possible.

NOTE Today, the number of organizations operating globally and transforming to web computing is heavily increasing. To these organizations, the Internet is a critical resource. At the same time, performing business over the Internet increases potential vulnerabilities. Inadequate security is one of the biggest threats to an HA system and must be considered a major part of the HA plan.

Choosing an Internet service provider (ISP) is a big decision. Providers should be able to provide documentation of past performance and best-practice standards. Proper HA planning requires companies to choose two ISPs. When evaluating each provider, take into consideration location and what type of SLA it can provide. Depending on location options, one may be more limited than others, but the goal is to find two providers with geographically diverse networks. Ideally, it would be from two tier-one providers such as Sprint, AT&T, or Qwest, just to name a few. Each sends data out over different networks in geographically diverse locations. If purchasing Internet service from two smaller ISPs that in turn receive service from the same tier-one provider, redundancy may be hindered. One power outage or construction project that happens to dig in to fiber is all it takes for both connections to go down.

Management must decide if a company's staff or the ISP will manage the Internet routers. There are advantages to both depending on specific needs and technical staff. If the company's staff manages them, then they are responsible for all routing and configuration changes as well as maintenance and troubleshooting. This is usually the best option as it allows more monitoring and troubleshooting control which will likely be faster than what the ISP would provide. The downside is someone must receive and respond to alerts on a 24-hour basis. If the ISP manages the internet routers, make sure monitoring, reporting, and maintenance is covered as stated in your SLA. Unfortunately, this can be a time-consuming task, as a call needs to be made to the ISP requesting the change to configurations, routes, and/or request reports. With this in mind, response time should be weighed heavily when creating an SLA.

When multiple Internet circuits with multiple ISPs have been chosen, the next choice lies in how traffic will be distributed over the links. Network load balancing becomes an important concept to consider.

Figure 5.1 demonstrates network load balancing. External network load balancers work in the same fashion as the application load balancers. They are a central point that monitors upstream and downstream connections and distributes traffic evenly across all available paths. If one connection becomes overloaded or unresponsive, traffic is diverted to the responding links and load balances are clustered.

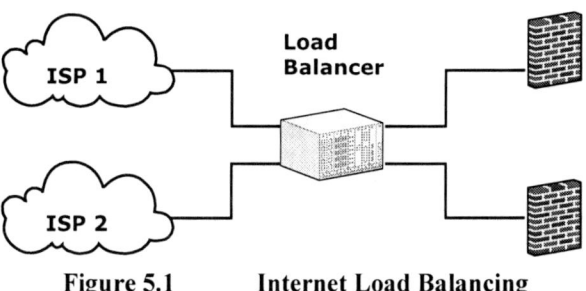

Figure 5.1   **Internet Load Balancing**

Routing and Switching

The routing and switching design of a high availability network may be the most straightforward part of the whole process. There should be no implementations of a single switch or single router when high availability is the objective. This goes without saying, but there are more components within the network to consider than first meet the eye. What about all of the Demilitarized Zones (DMZ) coming off the firewalls? All of the money that was spent on a firewall cluster can be negated because an interface from both firewalls is connected to the same single switch. Implementing devices with redundant power supplies that are connected to different power circuits is also an important consideration.

It may not always be necessary to provide dual switches in all instances, especially with some of the higher end models such as the large chassis products from Cisco. In one chassis, they allow for dual power supplies, dual supervisor or controller modules, and multiple modular blades in a nearly-limitless configuration of port densities, speeds, and media. With chassis switches, best practice dictates that servers or devices with multiple network connections be connected to separate blades in these switches. Whenever possible, it is advisable to provide two or more paths at any given point in a network. An example of this would be two routers running HSRP (Hot Standby Router Protocol) or VRRP (Virtual Router Redundancy protocol) protocols allowing clustering of the routers. They would answer on a single virtual IP address, which moves to the standby unit in case the primary should fail.

The more important consideration in choosing network hardware is capacity. Avoiding bottlenecking of a network is important. Caution should be used when calculating bandwidth requirements on hardware. If a network segment exists that has an average throughput of 10 GB of traffic, routers should be implemented that can handle better than 10 GB individually, not in aggregate. Otherwise, you will overload the remaining router in the event of outage. A year or two of growth may increase network utilization above and beyond what a single network device can handle. To prevent these situations, it is imperative to combine capacity planning with a strong monitoring and network management program.

A quality access and configuration management system for network hardware should be developed next. Having a centrally managed authentication system that allows for two factor or at least LDAP authentication is a necessity. This provides much tighter access control to the hardware itself and is a single point of account administration. This becomes even more important in large environments that may have hundreds of routers and switches making it all but impossible to manage individually.

Equally as important is logging. There are two types of logging to be concerned with. The first is administrative logging, which is basically a journal of all administrative functions or configuration changes that users perform on the device. The second is syslog, which can record all events from extremely detailed debugging information on each packet traversing the interfaces to critical system errors. Not only is syslog level information important, but equally important is administrative logging. Administrative logging gives users the ability to see what user account made a particular change on a device. That can be particularly important in quickly getting a piece of hardware back up in production as well as identifying any non-approved changes. A proper syslog facility provides an easy place to search when troubleshooting problems or potential unauthorized access attempts.

Configuration management is another point of focus. With potentially hundreds or thousands of network devices all requiring detailed configurations, it is quite beneficial to quickly be able to apply an identical configuration to a new device and have it back in production within minutes. Just as you would run regular backups of your servers, it is essential to backup router, switch, and firewall configurations for the same reasons. This can be achieved with something as simple as hand-written scripts or with more expensive and complex commercially available configuration management products such as Alterpoint.

Firewalls and Network Security

Proper firewall placement and design are your primary lines of defense. Without this type of security, malicious Internet traffic could flood DMZs and data center. As with other network hardware it is imperative to install firewalls in pairs. Whether you choose to use an active-passive or active-active configuration depends on your requirements and budget, but active-passive configurations suffice for most organizations. As with most modern firewalls, session state is maintained during failover with minimal to no packet loss. Some more common firewalls seen in the enterprise are Juniper Netscreen, Checkpoint, and Cisco Pix or ASA.

As with application design, there are three distinct layers to a secure network design. This is known as a three-tier network design as shown in Figure

5.2. The layers are the presentation layer, application layer, and data layer. Together, they look like concentric rings emanating from the core of your data center.

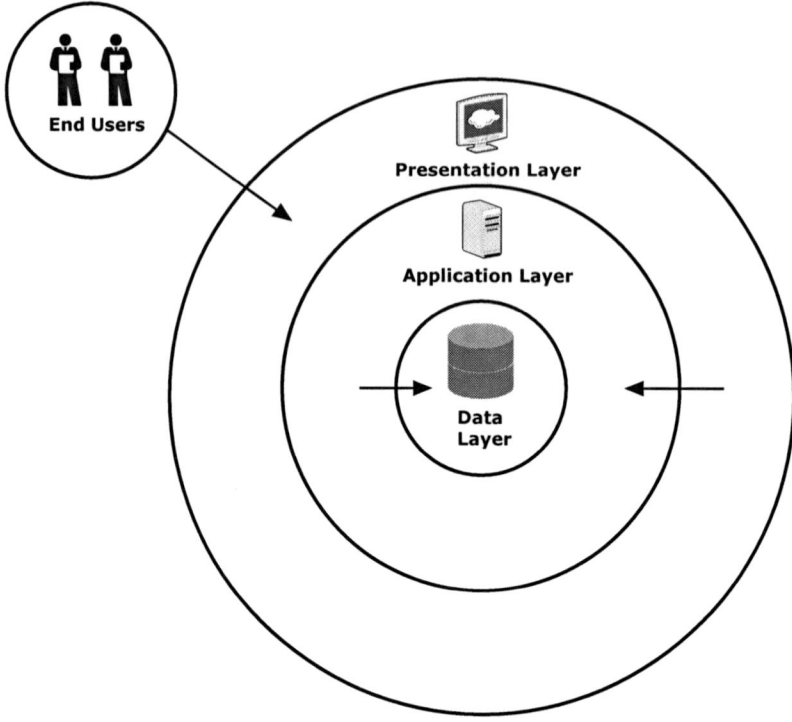

Figure 5.2   **Three Tier Network Design**

The core contains the data layer, which refers to your highly protected databases and data repositories. The data layer contains the mission-critical information that powers your organization and should reside behind a firewall, and quarantined from the rest of your network. The only traffic that should be allowed to that portion of the network is requests from application servers that are specifically permitted by the firewall. No direct user sessions should be allowed at this core level; remember you are protecting your organization's core assets. If an attacker, errant user, virus, or any other malicious traffic corrupts or hinders that data, availability will be compromised.

Next is the application layer which resides between core firewalls, protecting the data layer and your perimeter firewalls. It could also be an interface or DMZ off of the core or edge firewalls with a purpose to house application servers. Examples are Tomcat and Websphere servers which take requests from the presentation layer or web servers and, in turn, process the data requested from data layer servers and return data to the presentation layer to fulfill user requests. This zone should only allow requests from the presentation servers inbound to the application servers, which are then allowed to query the back-end data layer servers. There should be very few to no user sessions with direct access to this layer.

The final layer is the presentation layer which would be a DMZ interface on the perimeter firewall. This could be for web servers that require access from the internet or completely internal DMZs for Citrix servers or other front end servers. User sessions would be allowed into this layer on specific ports such as 80 and 443 for web traffic. Presentation layer servers would then be granted specific port and IP address access to only the necessary application layer servers.

A strict business policy should be enforced that only allows specific access through a firewall. In other words, blanket access for all IP addresses or all ports should never be allowed. It is highly preferable to limit access to specific source IP addresses going to specific destination addresses and only over a particular port or protocol. Once again, the goal is to keep out any traffic or limit the potential for traffic that could harm your availability.

One final product to investigate is a network intrusion prevention solution. This is a device that resides inline at key points in a network and inspects traffic for malicious or unwanted traffic. This type of device can be very effective in alerting and defending against virus traffic as well as mitigating denial of service attacks. Since these are rule-based devices and can be tailored to individual environments, companies choose whether to drop malicious traffic or simply send pages and alert on the traffic according to their preferences.

DNS

Domain Name Server (DNS) is a network service and needs special mention because of its criticality to the availability of a networked environment. Since DNS provides the name resolution for all Internet facing applications and web addresses won't resolve without it, it is a very critical component.

ISPs have the ability to host DNS, or you may choose to host it internally. Both have advantages and drawbacks of their own. Most ISPs have large DNS servers that are secure and already designed for high availability. Taking requests and adding zones or records at your request, ISPs are an easy and reliable solution for an organization that has a small number of domains or rarely requires changes to DNS. If regular changes or added zones and domains occur regularly, then the hassle of submitting requests and waiting for the ISP to implement them may be inadequate.

Large organizations usually choose to host their own DNS. This allows for quicker response time and more flexibility when making changes or additions to DNS. While these are great benefits, internal hosting is complex. Since DNS is critical to the web infrastructure, one must design a DNS infrastructure that is resilient and can withstand the plethora of DNS exploits and hardware failures that commonly occur. This can be handled with a few steps such as providing a hardened server environment with jailed processes and staying up to date on patching levels. It is preferable to run DNS services (commonly BIND in a UNIX or Linux environment) while depending on the expertise available on those platforms and your ability to keep them patched. An alternative would be to use a commercially available, purpose-built appliance such as InfoBlox or BlueCat Adonis. The devices are hardened, secured, and provide easy pre-tested patching, robust management and reporting.

A final and important DNS consideration is choosing between a master-slave or hidden-master configuration. The hidden-master is preferred because there is one master server that is protected on a trusted network and only provides data to the slaves as shown in Figure 5.3. This helps protect the integrity of your master server or servers. In addition, DNS servers should be deployed in geographically disperse locations. They should not be sitting side by side in the same data center on the same Internet segment. This decreases the likelihood of taking your entire DNS environment down.

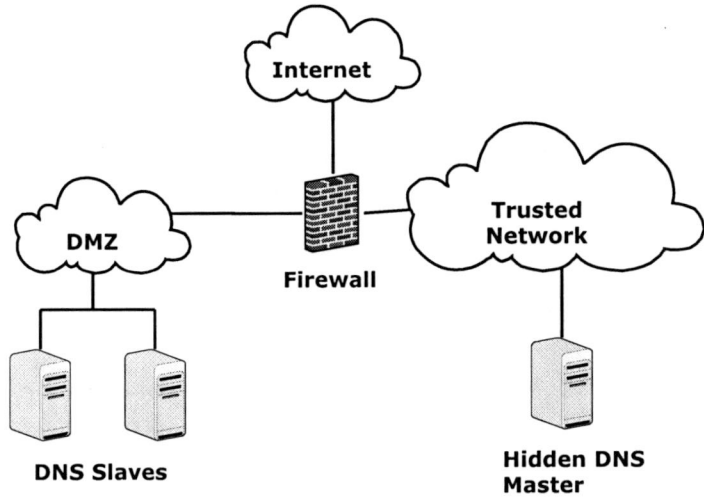

Figure 5.3   Hidden Master DNS

Network Management

As with other aspects of the network, companies may choose internal or outsourced network management. Whether internally hosting or outsourcing to a network operations center (NOC), the decision should align with the company's HA demands. As usual, both have their advantages and disadvantages. No matter which model fits your business, network management isn't an option, it is a requirement.

      The major advantage of outsourcing to a NOC is that networks are constantly monitored. NOCs report all network problems and initiate the resolution immediately after they occur. If preferred, the NOC will alert your internal staff and allow them to handle the issue. Chances are your IT staff will have other responsibilities than network monitoring, and/or you may have limited staff that cannot monitor 24 hours a day. Since that is the only task the NOC has to perform, it may be easier to provide a higher SLA with this method. Though outsourcing is convenient, the drawback is price. It can cost a premium to have a large network monitored 24 hours a day by a dedicated NOC; however, these premiums are often more cost effective than having less-experienced technicians dedicated within your own organization.

The other option is to provide your own network monitoring and management. Depending on the number of devices and circuits being monitored, this can be as simple as a homemade script that pings each device once a minute and triggers an alert if it does not receive a reply. If you have a much larger network, a combination of commercial products such as Solar Winds, What's Up Gold, Orion, and MRTG can provide monitoring, alerting, reporting and trending. If you choose to use this method, it will be necessary to configure your software to monitor and continually update each device, which will take considerable time in a large dynamic environment. Also needed is a staff that can receive these alerts and immediately react to them 24 hours a day. This includes remotely logging into routers to fix problems, contacting providers if it is a WAN or Internet link experiencing problems, or physically replacing a device at any time of the day or night.

As previously mentioned, there are more components to building high availability networks than simply installing two of every device. As important as the proper hardware can be, it is of equal importance to spend plenty of time in planning, device management, and studying reports and trending of your network. This is where you get the information necessary to plan for current and future capacity and how you learn where your infrastructure's weaknesses are. Simply getting better insight into the network you currently have can go a long way in improving your availability levels.

CHAPTER 5
REFLECTION

The network is the backbone of any system infrastructure that involves more than one computer. Carrying data between its sources and requestors, the network is the blood flow of an organization. As networks become more sophisticated, they are more vulnerable to various activities that can negatively affect HA and the integrity of your systems. Some key concerns include general security, malicious activity, and growing and sometimes unpredictable bandwidth requirements.

Take a few minutes to reflect on the following thoughts to help formulate ways to make your systems more highly available.

1. How reliable is your network? How often do you get complaints from internal and external customers? Chances are most complaints involve availability and performance. If performance has been an issue, is it a symptom of unavailability?

2. If you lose your primary Internet connection, what is your contingency plan to communicate with the outside world?

3. How critical is email and electronic data transmission to your organization? If critical, an optimal network HA solution is crucial for those systems.

4. How embedded and protected is your critical data within your network? Is your data isolated from public access? Is it really protected?

5. If you do not outsource to a Network Operations Center (NOC), what compromises may you have made in terms of HA, security, or personnel expertise/availability? Remember to weigh perceived cost savings with the costs associated with unavailability.

Chapter 6: Employing and Managing HA

Successful HA environments depend heavily on the right management process. As mentioned throughout this book, availability of information systems is one of the most significant aspects to any service industry in today's data-driven world. Management methodologies and technical staff play a crucial role in implementing and maintaining a highly available systems environment. Service levels and risk awareness are prominent elements in measuring and evaluating availability.

Having a well thought out approach will ensure a maintainable HA environment. This chapter identifies some of the most common methodologies and personnel requirements that best support planning and managing an HA environment. Additionally, this chapter discusses the importance of personnel, required expertise, and post-implementation management.

Methodologies to Employ and Manage HA

Several good management methodologies and models exist today that can assist in defining HA requirements. It is important to have an understanding of each, as they all play a role. Using a methodology provides the most educated approach. More importantly, HA services require a top-down commitment from the leadership of the organization. Without their commitment, HA obstacles can be difficult to overcome, especially when dealing with cost. Care must also be given to availability management. Although management of tasks is similar to standard system management, an availability management approach has additional service level requirements.

Figure 6.1 illustrates how methodology bridges the multiple gaps between the plan and successful execution.

Figure 6.1   The Value of Methodology

More than ever, organizations rely on IT services to assist in generating and maintaining revenue. Proven methodologies help the business and IT department simplify and streamline business processes. As organizations become more committed to technology, knowledge obtained from data becomes part of the business core. People, services, processes, and technology should all work together seamlessly to provide IT service, and methodologies provide a playing field for this critical collaboration.

There is an endless amount of information and guidance available to IT management. The following are the most commonly used methodologies that support HA.

- Service Continuity Management (SCM)

- Service Level Management (SLM)

- Configuration Management (CM)

- Project Management Planning (PM)

- Life Cycle Management (LCM)

Service Continuity Management (SCM) is an approach to maintaining continuity of service. It is proactive and reactive in nature. SCM encourages proactive assessment of service needs that support HA efforts and reduces risks that can disrupt continuity. Recovery is a reactive process that handles disruptions when they occur. SCM includes taking additional programmatic measures in hardware, software, and service. Hardware and software can be engineered to better support HA by identifying possible risks, designing around them, and creating additional processes to handle disruptions. Service processes are also analyzed to offer additional proactive means to continued service.

Service Level Management (SLM) is the process of delivering and maintaining IT services. Service requirements are identified to calculate the service level and cost to maintain that level. To better support the service-level requirements, it is necessary to analyze the impact to business for failed IT services. This involves hardware, software, and service. Once a service level analysis is complete, a level of service can be established and agreed upon between the customer and service provider in the form of a Service Level Agreement (SLA). Procedures are then constructed to support the SLA.

Configuration Management (CM) is the methodology used in managing changes that occur throughout a system's life. CM identifies a set of activities that control the change by identifying the items likely to change, identifying the relationships among them, and defining mechanisms for managing the change. Whether there is a new software release or just a fix to a software bug, CM ensures an effective and careful approach in making change and reducing risk of residual problems. Without a solid CM approach, risk increases. CM is an important piece in providing highly available environments. Processes and procedures that enforce effective CM reduce the overall risk of failure.

Project Management Planning (PMP) is a group of concepts used for control, leadership, teamwork, and resource management that helps create a successful project. Effective project management planning is a management concept that can assist in achieving highly available systems. Through detailed planning, quality assurance, performance measurement, cost management, change management, and time management, the risk of failure is decreased and the probability of success is vastly increased. Good project management practices produce a better product at a lower cost and with a greater return on investment.

Life Cycle Management (LCM) is the act of establishing management policies and procedures, design, development, deployment, operation and maintenance, enhancement, and retirement of a system. The primary objective of this approach is to deliver quality systems on time that meet expectations and are within cost estimates. These policies and procedures should work effectively within the current and planned information technology infrastructures and be cost effective to maintain and enhance. Life cycle management provides a proactive ingredient to creating, maintaining, enhancing, and ending an HA implementation.

Table 6.1 provides a basic matrix that summarizes the application of common management methodologies in an HA environment.

Table 6.1. Common HA management methodologies

Methodology	Planning	Change	SLA	Risk	Continuity	Life Cycle	Management
SCM	x		x	x	x		
SLM	x		x	x	x		
CM	x	x				x	x
PMP	x			x			x
LCM	x	x				x	x

Other Management Models that Support HA

Various other concepts that support and add value to management methodologies include:

- Capability Maturity Model - Identifies best practices to help increase maturity of an application or environment.

- Capacity Management - Used to measure the current and future systems requirements. This is done by projecting system life cycles and data growth. As data grows and new applications come online, additional resources must be allocated or replaced with bigger and faster systems.

- Six Sigma - A disciplined approach and methodology for eliminating defects in any process, from those supporting data warehouse systems to those supporting transactional systems. It is a measurement of quality that strives for near perfection.

- ISO-9000 - A standard for management processes and organization that support the best practices in quality workmanship. This ensures the development and release of quality systems.

Qualifications of Personnel to Support HA

True high availability combines people and processes with technology. Retaining personnel with the knowledge to manage processes, carry out risk analysis, make technical changes, and develop plans is vital. Although an HA solution can exist without all three components, consideration to all provides enterprise-class availability in any environment. Without personnel in place to manage the solution along with the management concepts mentioned in this chapter, no real guarantee can be placed on the availability of your critical systems.

If your internal staff does not have the required qualifications to properly manage and execute an HA project, it is more timely and cost effective to outsource to an experienced service provider.

NOTE

Often, personnel skills and management are overlooked during the implementation and support processes of any business project. For projects as critical as HA implementation, only qualified engineers or administrators should be used. Utilize managers and engineers with strong backgrounds in enterprise systems. Together, the team must have solid network experience, strong SAN or NAS knowledge, concrete UNIX or Windows systems-level experience, database and web administration experience, and the capability of documenting the architecture along with a standard of operations. All these skill sets require experience with proven results. Additionally, vendor support is essential. In many cases, the vendor can quickly eliminate unknown problems that are encountered in any stage of the HA lifecycle, so a vendor should be called about specific issues that might take place. If a third party is chosen to help augment the current staff, request documentation and a transfer of knowledge.

CASE STUDY

Logistics Company

Paid to provide timely and reliable transportation for its clients, this logistics company relied heavily on the availability of its clustered database system. Scheduling pickups, deliveries, and recording transportation records, a functioning database is essential for supply-chain management.

Problem:

Increasing gas costs forced the company to increase its service rates. Unfortunately, the company lost some of its main clients to competitors and a surprise budget cut released many of the skilled IT staff. The surviving employees also left shortly thereafter citing no job security. Among the people to leave was the only remaining UNIX Systems Administrator. When he left, so did all the knowledge for managing and troubleshooting the UNIX cluster.

The company was left without any knowledgeable administrators, much less an individual with cluster experience. The company drafted an intelligent, yet untrained, developer to attempt to manage the cluster. This resulted in numerous failures where the HA cluster was down more often than it was up. What used to be an effective HA system was rendered an unreliable and expensive couple of servers. Needless to say, the remaining clients experienced late deliveries, improper invoicing, and unavailability of the online tracking system.

Lessons learned:

Ultimately, the system was replaced with a simpler solution that the junior technical staff could keep running but it lacked the fault tolerance the company required. The key underlying problem here was poor cost cutting decisions by management and failure to keep or train qualified administrators.

Implementing HA

With the right approach, people, and technology, implementation of an HA solution should be a fairly transparent process to customers and end users. However, even in the best-case scenario, road bumps can be expected. In order to help ensure road bumps do not become setbacks, the following items are provided to serve as a baseline for executing an HA implementation.

- Revisit the Service Level Agreement. Verify the accuracy of the SLA and make sure all HA ingredients have been included to support the SLA. Although the terms should be ironed out by now, it is easier to make adjustments pre-implementation that will support a higher service level.

- Make sure your implementation team is built, educated, and ready to go. Outside of a one-man IT shop, there should ideally be overlap in knowledge and responsibilities. Facilitate a means to share knowledge between team members, employees, and third-party consultants. Even if employees will not be involved in the implementation, they should be well informed and have a chance to buy into the plan since their cooperation will be required by third-party consultants.

- Implementation of some HA components may cause temporary disruption of service to the production environment. Ensure, whenever possible, that changes to be made to production have been tested with a favorable outcome. A certain amount of downtime during HA implementation may be acceptable; this is planned downtime. Unplanned downtime caused by HA implementation (the very thing HA is attempting to resolve) is unacceptable and will not be well received by customers and end users.

- Ensure adequate research has been conducted for all new technologies to be used. If vendors are involved prior to implementation, their ability to support an HA implementation is greater.

- Communicate all changes to production environments to applicable customers and end users. If people anticipate potential disruption in service, tolerance levels are much higher.

- Set realistic goals and deadlines. It is not worth compromising a mission-critical production environment to get a few days ahead of schedule. Poor planning or a single mistake can set a project back for months, waste valuable budget dollars, and jeopardize the success of the project altogether.

Managing HA

Ensuring high availability is completely a proactive process that yields maximum uptime of your mission-critical systems. Despite the importance of availability and the dependence organizations have on their systems and data, proactive management is quite often not a routine process. Even organizations with complex HA solutions seem to struggle with the ongoing management of information systems. Many organizations, even after investing in an HA solution, gamble with their data. People tend to slip into a comfort zone until "something" happens. Unfortunately, a reactive approach does not support customer and end-user requirements for HA. Some do not understand the importance of proactive management, and others do not know how to execute. Three components comprise proactive management of HA environments.

- Proactive monitoring
- Routine maintenance
- Reactive support

Proactive monitoring should involve both automated and manual processes. Automated processes should be configured to perform all basic and mundane monitoring 24/7. Automation may involve custom programs and scripts or third-party products. Even for systems that operate only during business hours, if off-hour monitoring is not in place, a critical system can be down for several hours on a Monday morning. Automated processes should have an alerting feature to notify on-call technical staff of problems or, better yet, potential problems. Identifying and resolving potential problems increases the likelihood that actual problems will not occur. Although the majority of proactive monitoring can be automated, there is no replacement for manually spot-checking systems on a daily basis. Proactive monitoring is a fundamental step in ensuring availability.

Routine maintenance must be performed on a regular basis. Some organizations require production system availability at all hours, but designate a window of time in which system maintenance can be performed. Maintenance is a critical time to replace hardware components, patch software, fix bugs, and handle important but non-critical issues discovered during proactive monitoring. Security threats and degrading performance are maintenance issues that can have a serious impact on a production environment. Although the window may be limited, it is important to chip away at the many maintenance tasks at hand. Prioritizing tasks that have the most impact on HA will help justify allocation of time needed. No matter how much time is allocated, take advantage of it to minimize problems and maximize availability.

Finally, an efficient method must exist for reactive support that meets or exceeds SLA requirements. Some organizations outsource to an IT service provider. Some invest in internal staff and have a rotational on-call schedule. Regardless, it is important to ensure that procedures exist for reacting to proactive alerts and emergencies according to customer and end user expectations. Upon notification, it is important for the technical team to not only respond quickly, but have a qualified person to dispatch to the situation. How an organization reacts to system issues is paramount in HA management; consequently, if proactive monitoring and routine maintenance are priorities, more manpower will be available for reactive support.

NOTE Many organizations outsource routine system maintenance. Some IT service providers offer 24/7 proactive monitoring, basic maintenance, and reactive support at a fraction of the cost of a full-time employee. Organizations take this approach to augment its own IT staff, and cost-effectively acquire 24/7 support, holiday support, and vacation support with near immediate response time. For organizations with production environments that must be highly available, outsourcing proactive monitoring and maintenance provides best value in terms of continuity, higher levels of diverse expertise, and responsiveness. As a result, internal IT staff has more time to focus on using technology to better meet business goals set by upper management.

Communication, Knowledge Transfer, and Transition

Regardless of the team used to implement and support an HA solution, a consistent level of system knowledge must exist. In addition to conducting a transfer of knowledge, experts on the team should be able to communicate using common language between technical and non-technical stakeholders. It is also imperative to ensure that roles and responsibilities of all parties involved in an HA plan are clearly defined and communicated. This is especially important if any level of matrix support, such as third-party consultants, exists. As with any team that intends to be successful, clear communication channels are vital.

Data, organizations, business plans, and customers' needs change. Something else that is inevitable, and must be factored into the communication equation, is your team changing. Especially in IT, transition of staff is a way of life for some organizations. A clear transition plan must be established to foster transition. If the HA project manager leaves the organization, who will take over? How will the replacement be trained? How long will it take to get up to speed? What has been done to ensure knowledge stays within the organization regardless of personnel changes? Any staffing changes have the potential to pose a serious threat to the success of any HA environment and must be part of the HA plan since management of an HA environment ultimately depends on the personnel supporting it.

 **NOTE** Change is inevitable. Business, system, and personnel needs will continue to transform as technology matures. Transition planning is a critical ingredient to HA planning. By having a transition plan, you maximize the knowledge that remains within your organization when people leave. As business and system needs change, it is easier to adapt while ensuring maximum system availability.

Documentation

Documentation is one of the final and most important deliverables of any project but is often the most neglected. Although documentation is a final deliverable, it's not one of the last tasks. Effective documentation is a work in progress and should be started at the beginning of the HA project. At a minimum, HA documentation should include:

- HA planning and design documents

- System infrastructure diagram clearly showing all touch points of the systems that may exist in an organization

- Contact information for all HA project team members, including vendor support information

- Backup and recovery plan with clear instructions

- Disaster recovery plan with clear instructions

- Documents that define organization and customer expectations, such as SLA

- Transition plan

- HA management procedures

CHAPTER 6
REFLECTION

As with any technology solution, HA requires strong collaboration between people, processes, and technology. Basic project management, among other methodologies, are critical to the success of any HA implementation. Once an HA solution is in place, ongoing management is of equal importance, and knowledge retention within your organization is non-negotiable.

Take a few minutes to reflect on the following thoughts to help formulate ways to make your systems more highly available.

1. Who in your organization is ultimately accountable for system availability? Does that person have all the tools and resources necessary to successfully implement and manage HA?

2. Who will be implementing HA? If an external source, what is your plan to bring the necessary knowledge in-house following the implementation? If internal, what is the plan to retain that HA knowledge?

3. Which management methodologies covered in this chapter best apply to your organization?

4. As your business and system needs change, how might you best adapt your HA plan in terms of planning and management?

5. As people transition in and out of your organization, how will HA be affected? What can you do to minimize impact due to personnel transition on the continued success of your HA solution?

CHAPTER 7: DISASTER RECOVERY PLANNING

Disaster Recovery Planning (DRP) is a topic that most organizations are aware of and concerned about, yet are sadly unprepared for. In the wake of recent natural disasters, awareness has increased, but implementing a plan within the organization is still lacking.

Disaster Recovery Planning specifies what an organization does when a disaster occurs. Some entities are mandated to have DRP plans or a Continuity of Operations Plan (COOP) for government agencies. However, for most organizations, this is not the case. DRP is something that does not get the attention it deserves until after something bad happens, typically because people do not realize the ramifications of a disaster.

If a computer system goes down for an extended period of time, the results can be devastating. The impact of an unavailable system could include:

- Loss of business in the short term while the system is unavailable
- Loss of customers to competition as the services remain unavailable
- Impact to a wide geographic region far outside the scope of the disaster area
- Impact to other industries and systems that are dependent on the down system
- Legal and government action if critical data or services are lost
- Disservice to the public at large if the system supports a mission-critical operations such as medical, emergency, water, or power systems
- Eventual failure of the business or organization

Despite these risks and the attention given to DRP systems, very few organizations would recover if a disaster occurred. Reasons for this include the "that can't happen to me" syndrome, poor or unrealistic DRP planning, and a failure to realistically implement and test the DRP plan. This chapter defines what the risks are and how to develop and test a realistic plan for DRP.

Types of Disasters

While it is impossible to plan for every possible disaster that can occur, it is important to identify the most likely risks to your system. This will allow you to establish contingency plans for when problems do occur. The first step is to identify the most common threats. These can be broken down into three general categories:

- Natural and environmental
- Hardware and infrastructure
- Manmade

Typical natural disasters in DRP situations are not terribly difficult to imagine. A flood, tornado, hurricane, or earthquake could destroy a company. Natural disasters have the ability to not only destroy the computer room but also the rest of the site. For that reason, the DRP should not only give consideration for the computer system but also for the people and any other business units that might be impacted.

Environmental disasters do not receive much attention from non-technical people but are far more common given the relatively delicate nature of computer and network hardware. Something could happen to render your computer room unable to support the computer systems stored inside. Examples include a water sprinkler system being triggered or a water pipe busting and flooding the computer room. Or the heating and cooling system could fail, causing servers to overheat and malfunction or even shutdown. For example, a construction worker somewhere could cut a power or telecommunications line supporting your computer room.

CASE STUDY

Small Internet-based Company

Primarily serving online customers, this company required nothing more than a small business office attached to its warehouse that processed and shipped orders. The office housed enough room for the four employees and included a computer room that was little more than a walk-in closet. Various Windows servers and small UNIX servers were contained in the room and all were hooked up to a backup power supply.

Problem:

One Friday afternoon, a strong thunderstorm knocked out the building's power. As planned, the servers stayed up due to the backup power supply. Power to the building was restored in a few minutes, and everyone left for the weekend thinking all was okay. Unfortunately, no one noticed the air conditioning system wasn't restarted. Over the weekend the temperature inside the sealed computer room rose to well over 100 degrees. At that point, the servers overheated and crashed/shut themselves down. No one had actually tested the automated pager notification system to let the IT staff know there were problems and this process also failed. Horrifically surprised Monday morning, the company discovered that its system had actually been unavailable all weekend, users and customers were unhappy, and operations were at a standstill until all systems could be successfully restarted.

Lessons learned:

A properly designed disaster recovery plan identifies all areas that could be affected by a disaster. By understanding the sensitivity of systems, organizations can better plan how to avoid risks such as overheating.

Hardware or system failures should generally not cause DRPs to be enacted, but sometimes they do occur. Here we are talking about a relatively simple event like a failed disk drive escalating into a full-blown disaster. For various reasons, sometimes a computer system will encounter a failure that the technical staff just cannot recover from in an acceptable amount of time. For example, a server may suffer a hardware failure that will take longer to fix than enacting the DRP. In those cases, it may make sense to implement a limited DRP until the normal production system is recovered.

Manmade disasters may be intentional or accidental. Intentional manmade disasters such as bomb or arson capture the headlines, or they may be more subtle like a hacker or disgruntled employee corrupting data. Depending on the situation, there may be legal, evidence preservation, and security issues that must be considered during the DRP implementation. In the event of a hacker or disgruntled employee, the integrity of any data and software backups should be questioned. Of all the types of disaster recovery situations, intentional manmade disasters can be among the most frustrating to recover from due to their very nature.

Accidental manmade disasters will sometimes happen by the most careful and best employees. It is important to fix the problem first and then determine the actual cause of the disaster and take proactive measures to avoid reoccurrences. The best course of action is to have safeguards in place to ensure accidents do not happen. These include having well-established development, test, and highly regulated and restricted production environments. Production upgrades and maintenance operations should be carefully planned, reviewed by coworkers, and tested prior to implementing in production. Before a system is upgraded, there should be a valid backup taken and a plan in place in the event that something goes wrong.

Develop the DRP Objectives

A DRP is an ambiguous practice. Developing a good DRP document is even more critical given that in a true disaster, key people familiar with the normal system may not be available. Moreover, those implementing the DRP may be under stress and more prone to make mistakes.

For a possible DRP situation, it is important to consider scope, time until redeployment, how fast systems must be recovered, allowable downtime, and how recent the data in the system must be. First, identify truly critical systems. For example, development and test systems are not critical and do not need to be recovered immediately in a real disaster. The focus is on the production systems and often which production systems. Not all production systems have the same level of importance. A web-based system hosting thousands of customers is more important than a system that generates occasional reports for management. The complexity and size of the systems in your DRP must also be considered. A small web server with static web pages will be much easier and faster to recover than a terabyte-sized database.

DRP Development

The following steps should be taken in the development of a DRP:

1. Identify how fast the production system must be recovered. Be realistic in your requirements. It is important to separate wants versus needs. Keep in mind that this is disaster planning if your primary site is effectively destroyed; there will likely be structural damage, people may be hurt, and legal issues may come into play. This is a step beyond normal HA planning, where we are guarding against normal hardware/software failures. Having said that, is it really necessary for your systems to be available to the public (who themselves may be encountering a disaster) in minutes or hours? Many organizations expect a recovery of their key systems in a true disaster situation to be within 24 hours.

2. Define what the degree of data concurrency must be between the destroyed production system and the newly recovered system. Again, while it would be preferable for the recovered data to be exactly as it was in production, it is important to be practical. Technologies exist to keep the data at DRP sites in synch but can be more complex and expensive than what is really needed. Many organizations are content with using the data from tape backups that are stored offsite. These may be one day to one week old. For those systems that require up-to-date data, there are options available that involve data replication, standby databases, or disk mirroring technologies.

Table 7.1 highlights differences between maintaining low and high data concurrency.

Table 7.1   Maintaining Data Concurrency

Low Data Concurrency	High Data Concurrency
Asynchronous data transfer	Synchronous data transfer
Tape backups manually moved between sites	Real time, automated data replication between sites
FTP or manual movement of data tapes	Automated data replication, database replication, standby databases, disk mirroring
Conceptually simple to establish and maintain	Technically more difficult to establish and maintain
Lower cost to establish and maintain	Higher cost to establish and maintain
Slower recovery time in event of failure	Rapid recovery time in event of failure

3. Identify what the performance capacity of the restored system must be. Many organizations just want their key systems to be up after a disaster. If they are somewhat slower than the old production systems, or not 100% as functional, that may still be okay. It is a common practice to use older hardware as the basis for the DRP site to keep costs down. As existing servers in production are replaced by newer hardware, they are moved to development/testing or DRP roles. This may be acceptable for some organizations while others have legitimate needs to have DRP sites mirror current production with current hardware.

4. Finally, determine what conditions must be present before the DRP is initiated. This decision ties into the list of threats your DRP was designed to encounter. For situations involving structural damage, the decision is simple. However, there may be partial flooding or sporadic electrical problems impacting the computer room. What if a critical database server has been down for a day and the technical staff assures management a fix is imminent, but the delays continue? Is it possible to initiate a DRP for a single system instead of a site, and what are the ramifications of switching back to the primary site later? These are questions that should be addressed when defining the scope and purposes of the DRP.

Figure 7.1 displays an example site strategy for a disaster recovery plan in a multi-site organization.

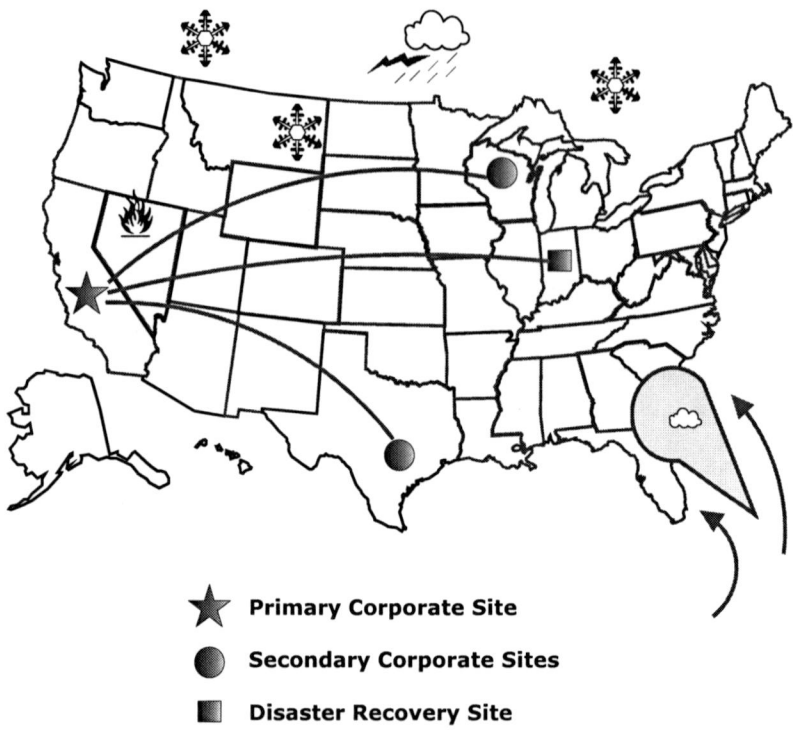

★ Primary Corporate Site
● Secondary Corporate Sites
▮ Disaster Recovery Site

Figure 7.1 **Disaster Recovery Plan Map**

Develop the Technical Plan

Once you have identified the systems to be recovered, how quickly they can be recovered, and the data concurrency, it is time to begin addressing the technical details of the plan. The first detail is to select a DRP site. This is a separate geographic location where the DRP computers are staged and prepared to be activated if necessary. This location may be owned and operated for a specific company or may be operated by a computer service provider specializing in DRP and supporting many different companies. The key necessities of a DRP site is that it have ample network connectivity, the hardware necessary for DRP implementation, and capable personnel onsite to provide basic hardware support.

Depending on the magnitude of disaster envisioned, to have the DRP site in another part of the same city may be sufficient. If a higher degree of protection is needed, the site could reside in another part of the country to avoid large-scale disasters.

After the DRP site is identified, the technical staff should determine what processes are necessary to establish the DRP system. They should know what systems to plan for in the DRP, the expected time for recovery, the data concurrency expectations, and how fast the new system must operate. They also need to know what the acceptable budget is for this implementation. This information drives technical decisions. Remember, the faster and more concurrent the recovered system, the more expensive it will be. Exceptional technologies exist for maintaining DRP systems but may be quite costly. For example, it is not unreasonable to use older hardware as the basis for the DRP system, as it is often already in the inventory. However, it may not perform as well as the equipment hosting your current primary system.

When establishing DRP sites, there are two general methods for keeping primary site and the DRP site synchronized: hot-cold and hot-hot.

A hot-cold site is where the primary site is up and running for normal operations (hot) and the cold DRP site is preconfigured but shut down and not kept in synch with the primary. Tape backups from the primary can be shipped to the cold site but they are not applied. In the event of disaster, the cold site receives the most recent copy of tapes available; they are applied to the servers and started up to act as current production. This is a technically simple way to implement a DRP. In this scenario, cost for implementation remains low. Negatives include the time to bring up the cold site and apply backup tapes plus the fact that backup tapes are most likely not current with the old production site data. However, for many organizations, this does represent a valid DRP solution. Figure 7.2 displays a hot-cold site.

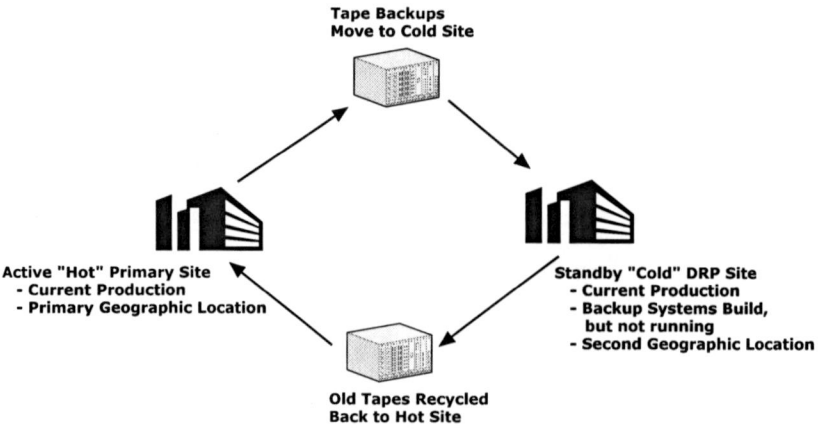

Figure 7.2   Hot-Cold DR Site

In Figure 7.2, we see a hot site where normal production runs with backup tapes being transported to the cold site in the event they are needed. The cold site is built to mirror the hot site, but is not actually turned on. As old tapes at the cold site are replaced by newer copies of production, they are rotated back to the hot site.

A hot-hot site is where the DRP site is kept up, running, and in constant data synchronization with the current production site. Automatic data transfer from the primary to the DRP site occurs at all times to keep the data in synch. That allows for a near-immediate failover in the event the DRP needs to be executed. Negatives include that these systems are technically complex to establish and maintain and are more expensive to support. For systems requiring nearly seamless failover, they offer the best solution as they are immediate to activate and have current data when activated. For added redundancy, note that tape backups are still rotated to the other hot site.   Figure 7.3 shows how the primary hot site has its data automatically transferred to the hot DR site so both locations are kept in synch.

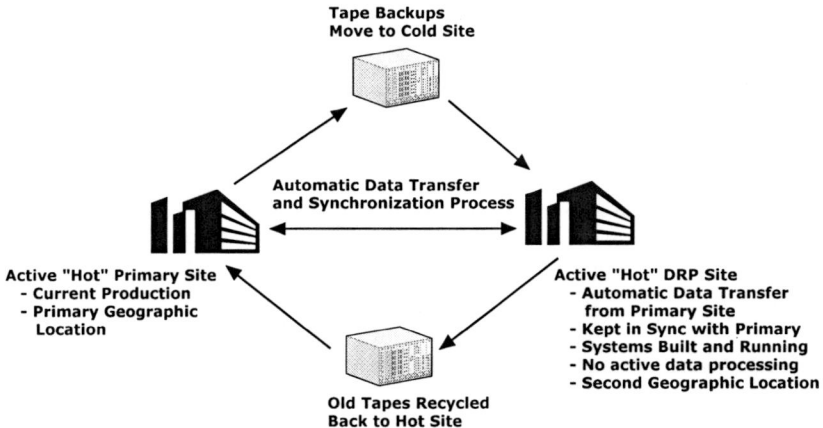

Figure 7.3   Hot-Hot DR Site

When developing the technical plan, it is necessary to step through the process to determine its accuracy. Make sure that no process or step is left out of the document identifying steps for the DRP implementation. Keep in mind the person actually using this document may not be familiar with the systems it covers. The technical staff that normally manages the primary site may not be available after an actual disaster. As a result, the implementers of the DRP may become whoever is available with the appropriate technical skills.

It is best to write the DRP document in a very detailed, yet simple manner so virtually any technical person can follow it. This document should be written by the technical staff that normally manages the primary site and then reviewed by other technical staff and management to ensure it is complete and understandable.

Implement the Plan

After the full DRP has been developed, implementation follows. This is when the actual DRP site is established, hardware and network infrastructure is installed and configured, and data and applications are initially loaded. The degree of preparation depends on the technical nature of the systems involved, whether hot-hot or hot-cold configuration is used, and the hardware and people involved.

Common technical issues associated with establishing DRP sites include:

- Insufficient network connectivity

- Network unable to handle user workload once DRP system is running

- Network is incompatible with backup tape drives or corrupted and missing backup tapes

- Lack of disk storage for the system. The primary site could potentially grow larger than the DRP site, especially if the entire space of the DRP is not monitored

- Hardware, operating system, database, web, and application software may not match the primary site in terms of base version, patches, or security patches. This occurs if the DRP site is not kept in synch with the primary for routine system maintenance

- DNS problems occur during the failover process from the primary to the DRP site. The network configuration and failover is an often overlooked part of the plan

- Network has difficulty reverting back from the DRP site to the primary after a DRP disaster

These technical issues can be addressed but some, such as hardware sizing or network throughput, may require additional funding to fix. It is also worth noting that once a DRP system is established, it requires regular maintenance to keep running. Routine software and security patches need to be applied in addition to keeping the DRP site running and functional in the event it is needed. This represents an additional maintenance workload on the technical staff. Historically, maintenance and administration of standby DRP systems is relatively low on most priority lists because they are busy supporting the primary system, so it is important to ensure these DRP systems are maintained.

Test the Recovery

Running regular tests of the DRP measures functionality, determines the time to implement, measures response time, and ensures that roles are understood by the staff. Improvements to the process and updates to the DRP documents should also result from these tests. Too often, organizations run an initial test after it is implemented but then fail to update written procedures for the invariable problems it encounters. Or organizations fail to run follow-up tests to improve processes and to keep people trained. Failure to run regular follow-up tests is a recipe for disaster; however, there are proactive steps to avoid this problem.

Every six months to twelve months, run at least one DRP walk through or tabletop exercise. This is where relevant participants simply go through the DRP document and rehearse their procedures in a role-playing environment. A moderator develops a disaster scenario (e.g. a tornado destroys the computer room) and then walks through disaster-recovery steps. This ensures everyone is aware of the DRP, their role, and provides an opportunity to make updates to the plan. Done in a day or an afternoon, this interactive exercise is much less expensive than running a full test.

At least every one or two years, a full DRP exercise should be performed. This involves copying the primary site to the DRP site, starting it up, making sure it works, and measuring performance and processing capacity. The only difference between this and a real DRP situation is that the primary site is kept running during the exercise, so there is not a service disruption for actual customers. It is important to keep this exercise as realistic as possible. Keep in mind that most exercises do not run smoothly the first time, and the process may need to be repeated until it is executed successfully. Once the test has been completed successfully, ensure the DRP documentation is updated accordingly. This test is more expensive to implement as it requires time from the IT staff, testers, and management to execute, but is the only way to ensure a workable DRP process.

CHAPTER 7
REFLECTION

How likely is it that a disaster will occur and disable your systems? Statistically, the chances are probably slim; however, disasters happen every day. If a disaster would happen to your organization, who knows if the result will be an inconvenience or total destruction to your organization, its mission, and revenue.

Take a few minutes to reflect on the following thoughts to help formulate ways to make your systems more highly available.

1. What types of disasters pose the biggest threat to your organization?

2. Do you have a DRP site? Do you store backup media offsite? If so, how quickly can the backup media be delivered?

3. Does your organization have multiple locations? If so, how can you capitalize on geography to better support DRP and HA?

4. Do you host your system elsewhere? If so, what is your vendor's DRP? Do you have an SLA? You are entitled to this information and it should be provided to you without having to ask.

5. Do you have a DRP? Has it ever been tested? How quickly can your systems be recovered in a disaster? Even if you don't have a DRP, try conducting a table-top DRP exercise just to see what comes up. This will at least begin to help identify vulnerabilities and get you going down the right road.

6. How important is data concurrency to your organization in terms of DRP? How quickly must data be available after a disaster recovery? How much data can you afford to lose and still continue conducting business effectively?

7. Would the benefits of having a hot-hot DRP site outweigh the cost and maintenance involved?

8. How detailed is your DRP documentation (if you have it)? The simplicity and appropriate details found in your written DRP will help ensure that you are actually able to rebound from a disaster, especially when some of your most knowledgeable systems staff may not be available post disaster.

Chapter 8: Balancing the Budget and HA

While budget is a major factor in determining the level at which a company applies its HA solution, the budget should not be arbitrarily constrained without proper analysis of actual HA needs. On the other hand, a budget should be wisely set and managed to maximize the benefit an organization sees via an HA solution. For example, insurance comes with a literal premium. A company could have all the insurance coverage available and never use it. In the meantime, premiums are dipping into potential savings or retirement.

Putting HA in place is like buying an insurance policy. The hope is that it never needs to be used but provides a safety net just in case. With the cost of implementing a full HA configuration being somewhat unlimited, it is important to weigh the cost with the probability and impact if something does fail. Assessing the risk and finding a balance between premiums and deductibles is important. Insurance is a good example because that is exactly what HA is. HA is an insurance policy to protect the availability of systems, thereby protecting the future of an organization.

An organization that chooses to operate without an adequate HA solution runs the risk of experiencing severe consequences and costs if unavailability occurs. This chapter identifies the potential consequences and risk of unavailability and discusses establishing a budget that balances risk and cost.

Figure 8.1 emphasizes that if risk and cost are placed on a scale, greater risk increases the required budget and lowered risk decreases budget.

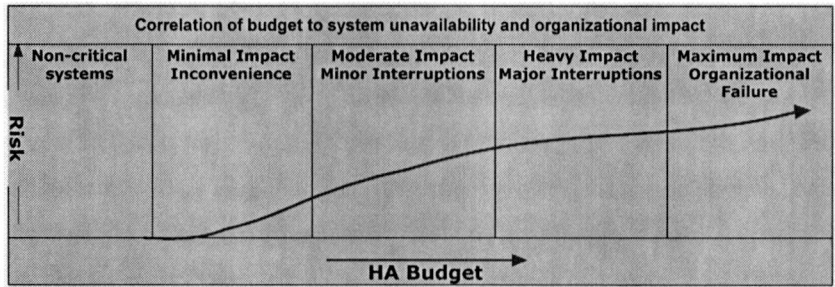

Figure 8.1   Balancing Risk and Cost

Stakeholder Buy In

As with any major undertaking, implementing an HA solution requires stakeholder buy-in for approval of capital and other resources. Obvious stakeholders include leadership and technical team. Other stakeholders may include end users and customers, depending on resources demanded from each and impact that may be perceived as negative during the implementation process. Table 8.1 describes various stakeholders in HA planning and implementation.

Table 8.1   HA Stakeholders

Stakeholder	Relation to HA
CEO	A vast array of organizational resources may be required to successfully implement an HA solution. The CEO should be aware of the required resources and prepare for temporary impact on customers, internal staff, and revenue.
CFO	The CFO controls organizational capital and must be convinced that an HA solution is worth the investment. The CFO needs to understand the costs associated with system downtime and the bottom line value an HA solution provides.
CIO	The CIO takes ownership of IT and must negotiate requirements and budget with the CEO and CFO. The CIO is highly involved in delivering on promises to customers and must bridge the gap between senior management, customers, and the IT department. The CIO will have the loudest voice in HA planning.
IT manager	The IT director or manager is responsible for planning and managing the HA implementation effort as well as maintaining the established HA environment. The IT manager needs to coordinate and manage any work performed by third parties.
Technical team	The technical team either implements the HA solution or works with the people selected to perform the implementation. The technical team is tasked with the ongoing maintenance of the HA solution.
End users	During implementation of any HA solution, end users may experience system downtime or temporary degradation in performance. Expect a temporary or perceived impact on end users.
Customers	During implementation of any HA solution, customers may experience system downtime or temporary degradation in performance. Expect a temporary or perceived impact on customers.

Meeting Minimum Requirements

Trying to determine what is needed and what can be afforded is usually a difficult process. Upon review, some components may not be worth the investment based on the level of risk that unavailability will occur. Two steps are involved in determining requirements for HA:

- Define the minimum requirements to protect the organization, support Service Level Agreements (SLA), and satisfy customers.

- Determine the level of HA that complies with the budget and offers the most value for the level of desired availability.

As previously mentioned, solid backup and disaster recovery plans must exist. These should also be a first priority. As far as defining minimum requirements, that is the purpose of the SLA. You may have a tailored SLA for each of your clients or business units that IT supports. Typically, SLAs are created under the consideration of how much money would be lost with a system outage. The impact could be from lost production of a product, processing order and shipping goods, and development time depending on your organization. However, if the cost of meeting these requirements was not considered when developing the SLA, the SLA should be reviewed and adjustments should be made.

Some of the key elements that need to be defined within the SLA in terms of HA include:

- Critical systems to support
- Critical hours of support
- Technical standards (system availability, responsiveness of support, and deliverables important to your organization)
- Service benchmarks and how they will be measured
- Consequences for noncompliance of SLA terms

After clarifying or revamping the SLA requirements, determine which systems are most critical to your organization. For example, if your organization processes medical claims, the most critical system would be the claims processing system. This system probably has the largest number of users, supports the most customers, and has the greatest financial impact. If your organization manufactures widgets, your most critical system would be one that supports the production line, allows inventory to be ordered, processes orders, and ships products. The importance of most other systems is secondary; although, multiple systems may have equal criticality.

Figure 8.2 shows common applications that are often considered critical systems.

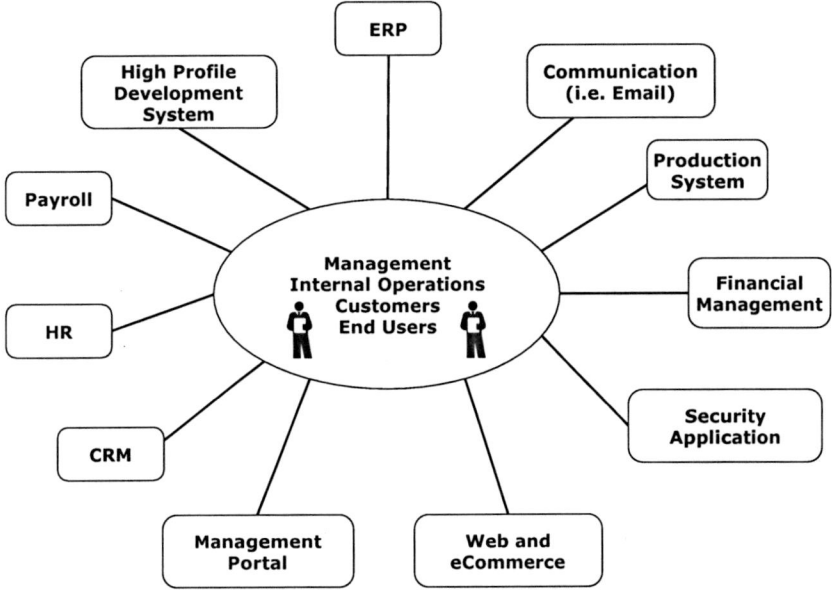

Figure 8.2   **Critical Systems**

Some other common applications that may require the highest HA levels possible may be security and payroll. Payroll is more obvious as you want to make sure everyone including yourself gets paid. On the other hand, if access to the corporate facilities and applications is controlled by a computer application, you want those applications to be available all the time. If the identity management system is down, how will workers access applications to do their jobs? If you have a revocation list stored somewhere and that component is down, is everyone kept out, or those with access and still in the identity management system still allowed in? The following sections explore potential consequences and costs of unavailability.

Consequences to Consider

Table 8.2 describes potential consequences and costs of the unavailability of critical systems.

Table 8.2   Consequences of Critical Systems Being Down

System	Potential Consequences	Potential Financial Loss
ERP	Inability to manage organizational resources	Loss of man hours and automation, impacting dependent systems
CRM	Inability to maintain customer relationships and target potential customers	Loss of customers, potential customers, and revenue
Production	Inability to create and move product, serve customers, and operate business units	Loss of customers, inventory, revenue, and man hours
Financial	Inability to manage finances, plan and forecast, and produce reports	Financial penalties, misuse of funds, angry customers, management, and shareholders
Communication	Inability to communicate internally and externally	Loss of productivity, customers, and potential customers
Web and eCommerce	Inability to serve, causing angry customers	Loss of orders, customers, and potential customers
Management	Unavailability of critical information for management decision making	Delayed decisions which could have high risk and costs
Security	Inability to enforce physical security and system security	Inability to access systems that have financial impact
HR	Inability to support, causing angry employees	Costs due to lack of recruiting and retention
Payroll	Angry employees, incompliance with laws and regulations	Loss of employees, financial penalties
Development	Development staff unable to perform primary duties, deliverables not completed, deadlines not met	Loss of man hours, projects fall behind, financial penalties for late deliverables.

CASE STUDY

Marketing Research Firm

Providing intelligence about products to large organizations worldwide, this marketing research firm required availability of systems 24/7.

Problem:

One day, the organization experienced production system downtime for three hours. After the system was finally made available, they estimated the downtime costs exceeded $100,000. Additionally, customer satisfaction and confidence in responsiveness was temporarily reduced. Estimated cost of reduced satisfaction cost the company well over $50,000 in just three short hours.

Lessons learned:

If an adequate HA solution existed and this organization had been performing routine monitoring and maintenance of the critical production system, downtime could have been minimized or avoided altogether. Chances are that an adequate HA solution would have cost considerably less than the loss of revenue from being down.

Perceptions are also formed when systems are not available. There is no cost associated with these perceptions, but you can count on lost revenue, lost customers, and "bad" word of mouth. Some of these perceptions include,

- Appearance of instability
- The organization is out of business
- The organization is not secure
- The organization cannot be trusted with personal data
- The organization is not technologically savvy
- Customer service is not important
- System availability is not important

Mitigating Risk

Before you can work to mitigate risk, probability of each potential risk to your critical systems must be assessed. What systems can afford to be unavailable for a certain period of time? What is your organization's tolerance for downtime?

Let's briefly revisit the insurance example. Table 8.3 uses fictitious insurance premiums to illustrate how people assess risk in terms of life insurance and how premiums are affected. As you can see, premium (cost) increases as risk increases. You might compare premiums to your HA investment and activation of an insurance payout to system unavailability.

Table 8.3   Assessing Risk for Life Insurance

Term	Coverage	Premium	Likelihood	At Risk Party
5 years	$500,000	$25	Very unlikely	Individual
10 years	$500,000	$50	Unlikely	Individual
25 years	$500,000	$75	More likely	More balanced risk
Life	$500,000	$100	Guaranteed	Insurance company

Table 8.4 lists common causes of system unavailability and the likelihood of each occurring. The same concept applies to system risk assessment as does life insurance, although there are many more factors and dependencies to consider in terms of actual cost.

Table 8.4   Assessing Risk of System Unavailability

Failure	Likelihood	Dependency	HA Investment
Power failure	Very likely- an organization has no control	Utility company	Mandatory for any level of HA. Invest in battery backups & generators for critical systems
External network failure	Likely- an organization has no control	Internet service provider	Invest in redundant Internet connections
Internal network failure	Likely- an organization has control	Internal hardware, software, vendor support	Invest in redundant network equipment and proactive monitoring
Hardware failure	Somewhat likely	Internal hardware, power, vendor support	Invest in redundant network equipment and proactive monitoring
Database failure	Less likely to occur with proper configuration and proactive support	Internal software, hardware, network, vendor support	Invest in redundant hardware/software and proactive monitoring
Application failure	Less likely to occur with proper design and proactive support	Internal software, hardware, network, vendor support	Invest in redundant hardware/software and proactive monitoring
User error	Likely- but usually does not cause major outages	End users of systems, usually internal	Invest in training for system users to minimize risk
Vandalism theft, and sabotage	Unlikely- but could be devastating	People internal and external to the organization	Invest in physical and system security mechanisms
Natural disaster	Unlikely- but could be devastating.	Weather, terrorism, etc.	Establish DRP and invest in off-site data storage and DRP site

How much risk are you willing to take? What is the likelihood and cost of potential loss of data or system unavailability? Can you afford to implement an adequate HA solution to protect your organization? Can you afford not to?

More than likely, an ample budget will not be approved to support an acceptable HA solution unless you get stakeholder buy-in. The only way to get stakeholder buy-in is by educating stakeholders on the risks looming over the company's information systems. A customer may not understand that brief power failure means that orders cannot be placed. A CEO may not fully understand the consequences of a natural disaster, and the CFO needs to see quantifiable evidence that the proposed HA investment will save the organization money.

Associating Unavailability with Cost

The following sections provide examples that help show how unplanned system downtime can be associated with actual cost. Although these examples use arbitrary numbers, hopefully they provide guidance on how to compute actual loss as result of system downtime for a given situation.

Example 1: Inability to Make and Ship Widgets

Suppose your production system supports the distribution of widgets. Let's say that every hour your organization ships 150 widgets, each at a wholesale value of $24.99. If your production system is down for a day or eight hours, the direct cost of not being able to ship your widgets during that time period is $29,988. An HA solution can help ensure that the system is always available. If eight hours of downtime only happens once per year and an adequate HA solution costs considerably more than $30,000 per year, it might make sense to risk not having an HA solution. Except that you also have to consider indirect impact of unavailability, such as missed deadlines, angry customers, and returned products.

Suppose we say that the indirect impact of system availability is $375 per hour (approximately 10% return rate of widgets due to missed deadlines). Table 8.5 provides a matrix that can help determine an appropriate HA budget.

Table 8.5   Establishing HA Budget for Widget Distribution

Downtime	Widgets not shipped	Cost per widget	Direct loss per hour	Indirect loss per hour	Maximum HA budget (break even)
1 hour	150	$24.99	$3,749	$375	$4,124
4 hours	600	$24.99	$14,994	$1,499	$16,493
8 hours	1,200	$24.99	$29,988	$2,999	$32,987
16 hours	2,400	$24.99	$59,976	$5,998	$65,974
24 hours	3,600	$24.99	$89,964	$8,996	$98,960
32 hours	4,800	$24.99	$119,952	$11,995	$131,947
40 hours	6,000	$24.99	$149,940	$14,994	$164,934

The following example is provided to make sense of Table 8.5.

- Estimated downtime per year without HA budget = 40 hours (example)
- Maximum HA budget per year considering risk = $164,934
- The key is to weigh the long-term impact of downtime against cost to make the best business decision.

Example 2: Unavailability of Web and E-commerce

Consider a highly active e-commerce application. It is available 24/7 for customer access on the web. Suppose that 100 product orders are placed per hour, with each order averaging $25. If the website is down for four hours, the organization may experience a loss of $10,000.

But consider that each hour 50% of the orders are new customers and 50% are repeat customers. Let's say that an average customer places three $25 orders per year; however, when the system is down, 10% of your repeat customers do not place another order that year. Consider the following math.

50 orders are from new customers, and the average customer places three orders per year. That actually equates to a loss of 600 orders over the course of a year at $25 each, resulting in a one year loss of $15,000 from new customers as a result of the four hours of downtime.

50 orders are from existing customers. If 10% of the existing customers do not place another order for the rest of the year as a result of being agitated with website unavailability, then that leaves us with the following conclusion:

- Loss of 50 orders per hour for 4 hours = $5,000
- Loss of 10% repeat orders for the year = $500
- Total loss from current customers = $5,500

Therefore, the total estimated direct loss as a result of four hours of downtime is $20,500. Again, indirect losses must also be considered such as angry customers, lack of word of mouth referrals, and so forth.

Example 3: The Importance of Email

Anymore, organizations cannot survive without email. When email is down, people have difficulty communicating with customers and associates. People are so dependent on email that many use email as the primary form of communication with their neighbor in the next cubicle. Whether right or wrong, our dependency on email has elevated it in to the category of critical systems.

Suppose you have 200 email users in your organization. Let's say that the average hourly rate, enterprise wide, for email users is $35 per hour including benefits and overhead. If email is down, let's estimate a 50% loss in productivity (varies by organization). That means that each hour email is down, $3,500 is going down the drain in lost man hours. If email is down for a full eight-hour day, your organization would be penalized $28,000!

Remember that there is indirect loss related to:

- Loss of contact with customers, which could exponentially drive the loss through the roof
- Loss of potential opportunities, potentially to never resurface
- Frustrated customers and associates
- Missed deadlines and deliverables

All of the different scenarios presented consequences could have been avoided by implementing a fairly simple HA solution and performing proactive system monitoring and maintenance.

Example 4: Financial Impact on Development Operations

When evaluating the cost of HA, production systems are most obvious; however, don't place the entire focus on them. If your organization is development driven, what is the cost of losing several hours or more a day for an application that is being developed or tested when a failure occurs? Suppose a major development effort is underway, and you have several of your own employees and many consultants working on it. Do they all have other work that can be done if the development environment goes down? If not, then there will be lost hours of production that still have to be paid for. The same scenario may also apply to major testing efforts.

Suppose you had a coordinated test underway with many of your end users. Some of the end users had to travel to another location for the testing. Therefore, you also have travel expenses as well as their time. For these reasons it may make sense to have some level of HA implemented for your development and testing environments. This doesn't mean that all development and testing environments need to be set up equally. Applications that are appropriate should be able to be moved in and out of an HA configuration in a fairly short time frame. Figure 8.3 illustrates potential loss in a development environment.

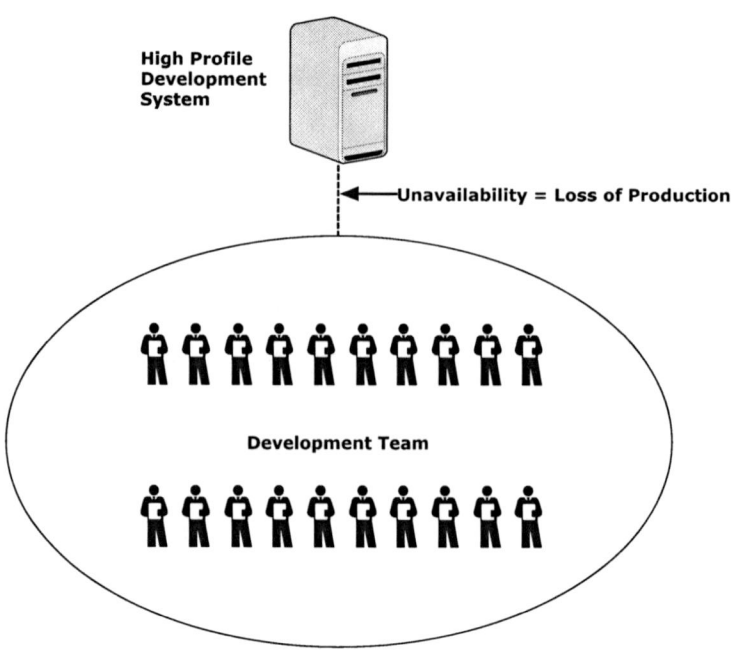

Figure 8.3 **Downtime for a Development Team**

According to the employment website www.monster.com, the average cost for a software developer is around $50 per hour, which includes benefits and overhead. Based on Figure 8.3, if the development system is down for eight hours, an organization would lose $8,000 in man hours alone with just twelve developers. If the development system is down for a week due to failure, you're looking at $40,000. Other losses to consider are:

- Incomplete deliverables
- Missed deadlines
- Project behind schedule
- Project above budget
- Overtime to catch up
- Direct impact on customers
- Direct impact on revenue

HA Accountability and ROI

Once an HA solution is in place, it must be measured. Organizational leadership wants to see that customers are happier and productivity is increased. The CFO wants to see a return on investment, meaning that system downtime is avoided, and potential losses are minimized if not completely eliminated.

Worksheets to Help Balance HA With Budget

Table 8.6 provides a worksheet to assist companies in assessing the most critical systems, dependencies, possible points of failure, and probability of failure. Using the worksheet provides guidance in selecting an adequate HA solution.

Each system that supports an organization has a unique level of HA configured for it. Besides the applications that are absolutely necessary, a monetary figure should be calculated to estimate how much money will be lost (i.e. via lost sales, productivity, and opportunities) from having an application down for some time. Companies should seek an HA solution with a cost that balances risk and probability of any potential failures identified. In the long run, an HA solution, while it may be costly, can protect an organization and allow it to operate more effectively and in a more profitable fashion.

Table 8.6   Critical System Analysis Worksheet

SYSTEM INFORMATION				
Name				
Describe				
Platform	Network			
	Hardware			
	Software			
	Database			
	Other			
Type	Development	Y / N	Production	Y / N
	Test	Y / N	Backup/DRP	Y / N
AVAILABILITY				
Describe				
Ops hours	Business hrs			
	Evenings			
	Weekends			
	24/7			
	Time zones			
	Maintenance			
USERS				
Describe				
Demographics	Customers			
	End users			
	Management			
	Web users			
	Time zones			
DEPENDENCIES				
Describe				
Demographics	Systems			
	Vendors			
	People			
	Nature			
	Other			
FINANCIAL IMPACT				
Describe				
Details	Revenue	Y / N	Productivity	Y / N
	Saves money	Y / N	Penalties	Y / N
	Man hours	Y / N	Other	Y / N
FINANCIAL IMPACT				
Public perception				
Security				
Safety				
Regulatory				
Other				

CHAPTER 8
REFLECTION

There is virtually no limit to the amount of potential investment for an HA solution. An adequate HA solution addresses single points of failure in critical system components and allows an organization to continue operating with little to no impact on operations, customers, or revenue. One must weigh the cost of all HA options and wisely invest in an HA strategy that provides failover for single points of failure without wasting valuable budget dollars.

Take a few minutes to reflect on the following thoughts to help formulate ways to make your systems more highly available.

1. Who are the HA stakeholders in your organization?

2. What is the potential cost of your most critical system going down? How long can it be unavailable before it really starts costing revenue, waste, and customers?

3. What consequences exist in your SLA for unavailability?

4. Do you have manual processes in place to compensate for unavailability? If so, what do these manual processes cost (more man hours, inefficiency, increased errors, etc.) as opposed to normal system processing?

5. What is the risk of temporarily losing a critical system, and what is the associated risk of losing revenue or customers?

6. What is the estimated cost of losing a repeat customer over the course of one, two, and five years?

7. What other direct or indirect costs will be assessed to your organization during times at which your critical systems are not available?

8. Today, web and email systems are critical for most organizations. Are yours critical? Are they HA?

9. Computing Return on Investment (ROI) can be complex and even different for most organizations. How might you measure ROI for your HA investment?

CHAPTER 9: HA AND REGULATORY COMPLIANCE

Organizations should not only ensure that their systems retain a high level of data integrity but also focus on guaranteeing that data is regulatory compliant. Regulatory compliance has become a necessary and integral part of disaster planning as well as a legal responsibility for many industries. The fines and penalties for noncompliance can total in the tens of millions of dollars, as well as possible incarceration for those individuals deemed responsible. However, regulatory laws and constraints are put in place for the well being of everyone and they should be viewed by companies as a positive and viable entity.

In recent years, HA and regulatory compliancy have not only grown into a practical relationship with one another but they also have an increasing importance with regard to anti-terrorism and national security. These new laws govern the accuracy of data your company maintains and the accountability of the system processing management that supports the data. Directly or indirectly, industries as a whole are legally melding under these laws and may be held responsible for the data they provide and how its provided in times of crisis. As an example, steel mills produce bar stock for the automotive industry, the manufacturer creates the vehicle, the wholesaler sells the vehicle to a dealer, the dealer sells the vehicle to the consumer, and financial institutions provide the funding for the purchase of the vehicle.

How many regulatory laws exist in the previous scenario? The process includes inventory, safety testing, employee, financial and accounting, and consumer data. Multitudes of complex data can be related together to form a complete and historically-accurate picture of how an automotive vehicle was produced and sold. What if this was not a simple family car but rather an aircraft carrier or a new life-saving drug? What would the consequences be if a seismic anomaly occurred during data transmission? What about a power grid failure? Is all of your data retrievable? Would there be a way to present a complete historical picture from start to finish?

It's easy to comprehend how important HA is to regulatory compliance and how companies must do everything possible to ensure compliance. In fact, many companies spend hundreds of millions of dollars to ensure it is in compliance. However, have these companies considered all aspects of data from a compliance standpoint? It is easy to focus on accounting, safety testing, or inventory data as being HA worthy; however, other "superficial" data lies within every organization that may need to follow regulatory compliance. One must leave no stone unturned to guarantee that everything possible has been done to secure as much data as possible in the event it may be needed to restore from a crisis.

Another point to consider is that the laws may tell what is expected from your industry in order to be compliant and the stringent regulations for noncompliance, but many laws do not disclose exactly how to achieve compliancy within your specific environment. Keep in mind that the various agencies which put forth these laws and regulatory constraints on a daily business are not out to ruin or harm a company. They are a necessary and valuable resource to make sure that we're all provided with quality products and services in our lives. To aid in keeping organizations compliant, agencies provide assistance by helping companies understand the laws and regulations, compliance audits, and compliance checks and balances for your company.

Ultimately, the HA plan your organization puts in place will aid in determining whether or not your organization is in compliance. As discussed earlier in this chapter, there are many issues and scenarios to consider. Below is a short definition of just a few of the many regulations that pertain to HA.

- Health Insurance Portability and Accountability Act (HIPAA) – Recording, storing, or transmitting patient data is regulated from the stand point that any changes must be recorded. Regarding high availability, companies who maintain "life safety" data must be available at all times in order to be HIPAA compliant.

- Food and Drug Administration (FDA) 21 CFR, Part 11 – This is a regulation set forth by the U.S. Food and Drug Administration regarding electronic records and signatures for validation of pharmaceutical data, documentation on computer system changes, and software, as it relates to pharmaceutical data.

- Securities and Exchange Commission (SEC) 17 CFR 240 – This is a regulation set forth by the Securities and Exchange Commission regarding the standards and practices of electronic securities exchange transactions and how those transactions are handled within computer systems.

CHAPTER 9
REFLECTION

In a world of promises, liability, security, privacy, rules, and regulations, it is important to make sure your systems are compliant with applicable government regulations, laws, industry standards, and basic ethics. This chapter provided an overview of the importance of regulatory compliance as well as a handful of common examples to which most organizations can relate.

Take a few minutes to reflect on the following thoughts to help formulate ways to make your systems more highly available.

1. Does your organization fall under the jurisdiction of any regulatory constraints or compliance issues?

2. Does your organization conduct business with the government? If so, more regulations and laws likely apply to you in terms of how business is conducted and how data is managed.

3. How will compliance issues affect your system in terms of HA? How will compliance issues affect the ongoing maintenance of your HA solution?

Chapter 10: The Future of HA

As technology accelerates, HA concepts must evolve in order to effectively support data-driven enterprises. Organizations are becoming increasingly more dependent on data and the technologies that are used to manage and turn raw data into knowledge and business intelligence. In the near future, HA will become even more critical as people have less tolerance "waiting" for data. With that said, the future of HA includes the following types of computing:

- Distributed
- Parallel
- On-demand
- Grid

Distributed Computing

By having many small, low-cost systems working together in a master-to-slave relationship, large scale computing can be achieved. In this scenario, a master or a few masters handle the distribution or replication of system environment changes. Mirrored systems in different geographic locations are updated or copied to the other slave systems. In most cases, operating systems and third party software products handle the changes. Linux clusters have made distributed computing an affordable reality. Additionally, hardware SAN technology is available to replicate data at the bit level. This is more widely used in a data HA solution.

Parallel Computing

In parallel computing, clustering software handles locking calls between multiple operating environments. It allows for multiple systems to work together to accomplish individual tasks. They can operate independently by updating the other systems through pinging or locking calls to memory structures. Generally, this is a master-to-master relationship with shared disk resources. These systems should be located within a close proximity of one another based on the large amount of network communication between systems. Oracle's parallel system (OPS), currently known as Real Application Clusters (RAC), has adapted well to be less problematic and easier to implement. Application software can also be written to take advantage of this concept.

On-Demand Computing

Standby architectures offer another method of HA achievement. Mirrored systems are used in a standby approach. If a fault should occur in one system, the other could be brought online to take over while the other is repaired. Sun cluster software and Windows Enterprise Server operate in this fashion. Both systems could be utilized in this model, but a less than 50% operating threshold should be applied. If one system fails, the other would take over and become 100% utilized. New methods have been developed to allow for more seamless failovers independent of human intervention.

Grid Computing

Marketed heavily by the database software giant Oracle, "grid computing" was originally coined by Carl Kesselman and Dr. Ian Foster of America's Argonne National Laboratory in 1998. Using an analogy between the computing power and the supply of electricity, grid computing delivers computing services whenever needed without the concern of where it came from. Systems can be added or removed, patched, and upgraded without affecting the overall grid. Usage of the grid would be charged by CPU cycles, memory usage, and disk usage. Much easier said than done, clustering multiple systems together with common process standards is far from perfect. Portions of this concept have been successfully implemented but not as a true grid environment.

A combination of HA concepts mentioned above could evolve in to one true grid computing solution in the next decade. Much work is still needed to standardize communication and protocols between systems. As vendors develop new and better grid techniques, they still have the issues related to proprietary systems. Utility companies running grid-type concepts are not bothered with conforming to another utility's methods. Instead, they share the same standards. Within IT, one architecture will sooner or later prevail and others will be forced to conform to one standard. Until then, revenue generating vendor grid-type solutions will be utilized.

CHAPTER 10
REFLECTION

The world has clearly become dependent on the Internet and a multitude of web resources that exist. Many businesses already operate on a web platform. With global communication made easy, barriers have been brought down for many. Is it possible that web computing is in your organization's near future?

Take a few minutes to reflect on the following thoughts to help formulate ways to make your systems more highly available.

1. As more organizations rely on global computing and the Internet as a critical business resource, what direction do you see your organization going? How vital will the web computing platform be for your organization, and how can it be used to more effectively provide data to your users and customers?

2. As your systems become more heavily integrated with web resources, what measures will be required to ensure adequate availability is maintained?

3. What threats are posed to your organization in a web computing environment? What opportunities exist?

Chapter 11: Common Mistakes

There are many misconceptions in IT, particularly in HA systems. To some, HA systems appear too complex and expensive to be deployed. Sometimes critical systems have a legitimate need for HA; however, either due to management or technical apprehension, HA is never implemented. Others assume that every system should be HA and that these systems are so simple to build and manage that anyone can implement them. In reality, not every individual system warrants an enterprise-level HA solution.

The truth lies somewhere in between these extremes of pro or anti HA. Part of the reason for confusion is due to the marketing hype associated with HA. A myriad of products exist which promise HA for virtually every implementation imaginable. Fierce competition erupts between vendors where products are turned out at a break-neck pace, where sometimes the initial releases do not live up to marketing's promises. Furthermore, oftentimes sales and marketing literature paints a very optimistic picture of how "easy and seamless" HA solutions can be implemented, which may not be the reality on complex systems. Technology vendors are partially to blame for some of the misconceptions regarding HA.

Another source of misinformation regarding HA often comes from the technical staff of organizations. This usually comes in one of two extremes: either the "techies" are enamored with the idea of HA systems and want to push the envelope of new HA technology, or they just want to get by with a simple non-HA system because they are unsure of the technology. In either case, technical details should be reviewed and tested before making a recommendation about a product. Given that a good deal of misinformation and misconceptions about HA systems exist, what is the best way to proceed? In an ideal situation, representatives from the business line should accurately present their HA requirements to IT management to develop an engineering solution to meet those requirements. The technical staff then examines solutions available based on the business requirements and makes recommendations to management with detailed technical pros and cons of each solution. Recommendations should include how the solution meets business needs, the proposed budget, and will perform for the foreseeable future. Management then makes a decision for the best overall solution and begins implementation. Unfortunately, proper analysis and decision making do not always occur. This chapter discusses those common misconceptions associated with the process.

Common Misconceptions

Below is a list of common misconceptions between both the technical and managerial community. Many of the items appear critical of HA systems but are actually attempting to state a reality often not realized until after an attempted implementation.

Misconception: HA systems do not experience failures like non-HA systems.

Fact: In reality, all systems encounter individual failures (e.g. disk failures, server crashes, etc.), but HA systems are redundant and hide these failures better from the end user. HA systems often experience more failures than standalone systems because there are more components that have a higher mathematical probability of failing. The difference is that because of the increased redundancy, HA systems have fault tolerance so the system continues to function despite individual failures.

Misconception: The new HA product is a "silver bullet" against downtime.

Fact: This is incorrect especially if the product protects only a single tier. Systems are composed of multiple, dependent components such as the network, application, database, and web interface. A failure in a component that does not have fault tolerance will result in downtime for the system. The cliché of chain being "only as strong as its weakest link" is true in HA systems.

Misconception: HA systems are easy to manage.

Fact: At best, some individual components are relatively easy to build and manage. However, remember it is necessary to have HA systems, not just individual components. While there are some HA products that truly are simple to manage, these are the exception.

Misconception: It is difficult to implement HA components.

Fact: Some components are more difficult to build under HA configuration than others. Some web application servers can be architected as HA in a relatively simple yet highly effective manner. However, many cluster and database systems are more difficult to implement simply because there are more dependencies and components involved.

Misconception: HA systems are complex

Fact: While sometimes true, a better way to phrase this is that HA systems are *more* complex than standalone systems. Most HA systems have additional processes that maintain synchronization and death detection among each component. It is very important for the technical staff to understand the differences between components in HA vs. standalone configuration, but this additional complexity does not necessary cause problems.

Misconception: It is too expensive to implement HA

Fact: Some HA systems can be expensive, but the price of downtime often will exceed the cost to implement HA. Some very reliable HA systems can be implemented relatively inexpensively, especially with Linux and freeware products. Other product suites can be more expensive, but many times organizations using more expensive products are the very organizations that cannot afford downtime. Therefore, they purchase more expensive solutions.

Misconception: HA systems do not deliver what they promise

Fact: The most critical part of HA systems are the people implementing them. If a smart and experienced technical staff has the opportunity to intelligently select, architect, and implement an HA solution, it will generally perform as promised. However, if the staff isn't up to the task, they do not receive the necessary architectural and infrastructure support, the project has unrealistic timelines, or the product suite is immature (buggy), the results can be less than expected. This last point is critical when addressing HA systems. Misallocation of resources occurs more often than HA systems that do not deliver.

Common Mistakes

Many of the best lessons come from failures. Often times, highly visible failures are the best teachers; people don't forget them. Below is a list of common mistakes that should be avoided:

Implementing an HA tool rather than an HA system: If only a single component is implemented in an HA configuration, the protection only extends to that component. If the majority of a system's failures can be attributed to a few individual components, then it does make sense to address those components first. However, the principle of shifting bottlenecks indicates that as soon as you fix the most problematic components, new problems will appear. Do not assume that by enabling HA with the current problem components, the rest of the system will run correctly.

Failing to implement an architecture that doesn't lend itself to HA: Poor server hardware and network topology decisions can render the most advanced HA software useless. Vertically scaling servers does often make sense from a performance standpoint but does not promote fault tolerance. Designing networks without redundant devices is a recipe for eventual failure. These types of architectural design decisions need to be made with HA in mind.

Failing to fully research the HA products available: There are many tools available to implement HA and assist with the management of HA systems. Furthermore, many products claim to provide HA but only under specific configurations. The cliché "the devil is in the details," is true in terms of IT systems. Before selecting a product, it is critical to research if it is applicable to the business needs. Be sure to examine configuration and implementation requirements, determine if there are required dependencies, product compatibility matrices, and purchase, licensing, and support costs. Also check outside sources for product reviews and the pros and cons of a product.

CASE STUDY

Insurance Company

With a growing population of Internet users, this insurance company was excited to hear about the newest web-clustering solution. Vendor-supplied white papers and demos sealed the deal as the company thought the solution was just what it needed.

Problem:

After purchasing the clustering solution, the company hired an IT firm to set up and configure the software. Within the first hour of service, the IT firm notified the insurance company that the newly-purchased software was not applicable in its web-server environment.

In disbelief, the insurance company showed the hired technicians the white papers and demos. Apparently, subtle differences existed between the application's technology stack versus what the vendor supported in terms of clustering. It turned out that the impressive looking diagrams showing clustered web servers were completely non-applicable for the vast majority of customers using that vendor's software. Only under a very specifically defined technology stack could the software be clustered as the vender described.

Lessons learned:

Needless to say, the client was not happy with this finding since the investment had already been made. The client learned to be more detailed in its research of new technology and knew what types of questions to ask next time.

Not testing the HA tools before production implementation: Most HA implementations are for production systems but, just like any technology, need to be tested prior to implementation. As many HA systems have complex configuration and management characteristics, it is important to develop optimized configuration settings, gain real-world experience, and establish best practices which can be done in development and test environments. Once the settings are established, prior to the production implementation, it is highly recommended to execute structured performance and failover tests to ensure the implementation performs as expected.

Not becoming highly proficient in the HA tools: It is the responsibility of the technical staff to become highly proficient with the HA tools they are using. There is a difference between a default HA configuration and a highly optimized HA configuration. Often the difference between a running system and a down system is the skill and knowledge of the technical staff running the system. There have been many cases where an advanced configuration or a technical "trick" has saved the day for a system. However, this knowledge is not developed within hours of a product arriving; rather, the technical staff needs the time to develop these skills and become authorities of the products they manage.

Not having staff skilled with the tools: There is a subtle difference between having a staff that is marginally skilled but not highly proficient and a staff that has virtually no knowledge of the HA software. Sometimes administrators are thrown in to situations where they have to manage complex systems with little or no experience. It is not realistic to expect success under these conditions; more often than not, the circumstances or management is more to blame than the technical staff itself.

Relying on "bleeding-edge" software: "Betting the farm" on a new, unproven technology sounds exciting; but in reality, it is risky and often results in failure despite the best efforts of the technical staff. The more complex and radical the technology, the greater the risk. Problems are exacerbated when the level of vendor support does not match what was promised. There are times when it pays to be the first to use a new technology but should be a calculated risk.

Not implementing an automatic monitoring system: A common mistake is to invest heavily on an HA system but not to implement an effective monitoring and notification system when the system goes live. A system that warrants HA technology usually warrants having a monitoring system that sends an email or pager alert to the on-call administrator if a failure is detected. There are many vendors that offer products which monitor its specific products and other components. Many of these products are highly customizable for what they can monitor and, in some cases, automatically fix. It is less important which product is implemented but rather that it is implemented in an intelligent manner.

CASE STUDY

Automotive Manufacturing Company

As a 24/7 shop, this automotive supplier realized the importance of HA and maintained a first-rate clustered system. Database administrators monitored the system by running scripts on a daily basis, plans and processes were in place in the case of a disaster, and the company hadn't experienced any downtime in over 11 months.

Problem:

One evening, the second-shift database administrator called off work due to illness. The IT manager approved the DBA's personal time but was unable to fill his shift. Knowing he had a reliable HA system, the manager left for the evening with no concerns. He had no idea that when he returned to work tomorrow the company would have already lost over $250,000 because of a script error that controlled the engine heat testing.

Lessons learned:

Various monitoring utilities (some freeware) exist to monitor server, database, application, batch jobs, and all supporting background processes. If configured properly, monitoring tools can be scripted to check numerous administrator-defined processes and send notifications to the appropriate administrator's pager. Based on the severity of the problem, numerous people can be paged. The person receiving the page would have to acknowledge the page within the system before notifications would cease. A tool such as this is very effective and saves money by reducing and preventing downtime.

For a 24/7, highly-automated shop, a more highly automated monitoring system would have prevented this disaster.

Not having a technical and management staff with the HA mindset: Implementing and managing HA systems are *not* the same as working with standalone systems. Supporting production systems is important and sometimes difficult, but HA systems are typically more complex, more highly visible, and require a real dedication for precise management. It takes a highly professional and dedicated staff to design, implement, and successfully support HA systems. These are not 8-5 systems; rather they are expected to be up 99% + of the time 365 days a year. That is not to say that a technical person needs to be watching the system continually as that is not practical. A better solution is a team of technically skilled administrators, a supportive management, and a mix of automated monitoring and administrative skill.

Many people are aware of the role of HA systems, but there are many misconceptions about what they can and cannot do. There are also numerous mistakes that are common among HA implementations. Despite this situation, there is a definite place for HA technology as it is responsible for keeping the most critical systems in the world running. Critical components for a successful HA implementation are accurate business requirements, intelligent architectural design, appropriate selection of mature technology products across all systems tiers, and effective implementation by a skillful technical staff.

CHAPTER 11
REFLECTION

As with any technology, it is important to carefully research solutions that will best support your organization's mission. This chapter unveiled some of the common misperceptions about HA as well as typical mistakes made while attempting to plan and implement such a solution.

Take a few minutes to reflect on the following thoughts to help formulate ways to make your systems more highly available.

1. What are the levels of HA awareness and experience that exist within your organization's staff?

2. Define your organization's objectives for an HA system. What are your customer's expectations for such a system?

3. Do you have confidence in your staff's knowledge and ability to successfully implement an HA solution?

4. Do you automate routine monitoring tasks as much as possible? Doing so is proactive, allows for around-the-clock monitoring at a minimal cost, and decreases the chance of important alerts slipping through the cracks.

APPENDIX A: LIST OF ACRONYMS

Acronym	Description
CRM	Customer Relationship Management
DMZ	Demilitarized Zone
DNS	Domain Name Server
DRP	Disaster Recovery Plan
HA	High Availability
ISP	Internet Service Provider
IT	Information Technology
NOC	Network Operation Center
RAC	Real Application Clusters
RAID	Redundant Array of Independent Disks
SAN	Storage Area Network
SCM	Service Continuity Management
SLA	Service Level Agreement

APPENDIX B: SERVICE LEVEL AGREEMENT CHECKLIST

Use the following checklist to begin creating a Service Level Agreement (SLA) to support HA.

Identify

- ___ Critical system components
- ___ Hours of operation
- ___ Hours of expected availability
- ___ Acceptable hours for planned downtime
- ___ Threats to availability
- ___ All parties involved in the SLA (customers, support staff)

Establish

- ___ Problem prioritizing system
- ___ Problem reporting procedure
- ___ Problem escalation procedure
- ___ Contact information (customers, end users, support staff)
- ___ Penalties for noncompliance
- ___ Accountability system (way to measure compliance)

Provide

- ___ Compliance reporting
- ___ Problem reporting and tracking system
- ___ Ongoing communication between customers and support staff
- ___ Means for easily adjusting SLA as needs change

APPENDIX C: SERVICE LEVEL AGREEMENT OUTLINE

I. Introduction

Purpose, objectives, parties to agreement, responsibility of parties, personnel changes, general contact information, general definitions, other pertinent background information.

II. Scope of Agreement

Who is getting the support, who is giving the support, services performed, systems supported, hours of operation, expected availability, allowable downtime, what is not being supported.

III. Duration of Agreement

Start date, review data, end date, option to extend or terminate.

IV. Service Provider's Obligations

Level of support, hours of support, response time, availability, problem resolution time, how system will be supported, frequency of monitoring, required reports, client-requested reports.

V. Performance

Key performance indicators, how performance is monitored, how performance is measured, tracking and reporting of performance.

VI. Problem Management

Problem definition and prioritization, problem reporting procedure, problem escalation procedure, problem tracking, closing problem tickets, how outstanding problems are handled.

VII. Remedies

Quality of service, limit of liability, penalties for noncompliance, cost reimbursement, early termination, restrictions, exclusions.

VIII. Legal

Standard legal language, confidential information, non disclosure statement, legal compliance, industry regulations, government regulations.

IX. Fee Schedule

X. Agreement and Signatures

APPENDIX D: SINGLE POINT OF FAILURE CHECKLIST

This checklist helps rate the most critical single points of failure. Complete columns 2-4 based on your organization's system environment.

Single Point of Failure Type	Component Name	Other System Component Dependencies	Criticality of Component (Scale of 1-10)
Internet connections			
Network connections			
Network hubs/switches			
Network load balancers			
Power sources			
Host servers			
File servers			
Database servers			
Application servers			
Domain name servers			
Data storage			
Databases			
Applications			
Backup devices			
Backup media			
Backup storage sites			

APPENDIX E: DISASTER RECOVERY PLAN CHECKLIST

The following checklist is provided as a tool to start a basic Disaster Recovery Plan. Complete based on your organizations' system environment and specific business needs.

Disasters Most Likely to Occur

- ___ Hurricane
- ___ Tornado
- ___ Earthquake
- ___ Thunderstorms/power outages
- ___ Flood
- ___ Fire
- ___ Security threats
- ___ Manmade disaster
- ___ Other _____

DRP Participants

- ___ Primary IT support team _____
- ___ Secondary IT support team _____
- ___ Primary organizational leadership _____
- ___ Secondary organizational leadership _____

DRP Locations

- ___ Primary production site _____
- ___ DRP site (secondary production site) _____
- ___ Offsite backup media storage _____
- ___ Distance between primary/DRP sites _____

Dependence on Data/Information Systems

___ Operations cannot continue without data

___ Operations limited without data

___ Operations not impacted by data loss

Most Critical Systems

___ Expected availability　　　　　　　　　_____

___ Expected recovery time　　　　　　　　_____

___ Geography of users　　　　　　　　　　_____

___ Overall impact on organization　　　　　_____

Data Concurrency

___ No affordable data loss

___ Can afford to lose *n* hours of data　　　_____

___ Can afford to lose *n* days of data　　　_____

___ Can afford to lose *n* weeks of data　　 _____

Post Disaster Recovery Performance

___ 100% functional

___ Partially functional　　　　　　　　　　_____

Testing

___ Table top exercise frequency　　　　　　_____

___ Full DRP test frequency　　　　　　　　_____

Documentation

___ Initial DRP documentation　　　　　　　_____

___ Ongoing maintenance of DRP　　　　　　_____

___ Personnel accountable for DRP　　　　　_____

GLOSSARY

Active-active – a configuration in which each node is actively serving the business applications and its users. In the event of a failure, part or all of the failed node's applications, IP addresses, and storage transition to the surviving node(s). All of the nodes in the cluster are utilized during normal production.

Active-passive – a configuration with a primary node that runs all of the applications while the passive node sits idle. In the event of a failure, the applications, IP addresses, and storage are failed over from the primary to the passive node and restarted.

Asynchronous data transfer – transferring data from one source to multiple sources in a sequential fashion.

Caching server – a device that stores graphical web content such as HTML pages, documents, images, or even fragments of documents so they can be quickly provided in response to incoming web requests, so the web server does not need to provide them.

Capability Maturity Model – an approach to identify best practices to help increase maturity of an application or environment.

Capacity Management – used to measure the current and future systems requirements. This is done by projecting system life cycles and data growth. As data grows and new applications come online, additional resources must be allocated or replaced with bigger and faster systems.

Clustering – the concept of connecting servers, databases, or applications to provide redundancy, failover, and increased performance. In a clustered environment, if one component fails, a surviving component picks up the load so processing can continue.

Cold backup – a system or database backup taken while shut down and unavailable to end users.

Configuration Management (CM) – a methodology used to manage changes that occur throughout a system's life. CM identifies a set of activities that control the change by identifying the items likely to change, identifying the relationships among them, and defining mechanisms for managing the change.

Continuity of Operations Plan (COOP) – another name for a disaster recovery plan that is commonly referred to in government agencies.

Data concurrency – the required level of synchronization between production data and data stored in a secondary database environment, or between production data and recovered data.

Disaster Recovery Plan (DRP) – a documented and tested process that enables an organization and its information systems to continue operating when a disaster occurs.

Distributed Computing – a configuration in which many small, low-cost systems work together in a master to slave relationship so that large scale computing can be achieved.

Domain Name Server (DNS) – a network service that provides the name resolution for all Internet facing applications and web addresses.

Failover – the process of a secondary system component being activated upon the failure of the primary component.

Fault Tolerance – the level at which system redundancies must be employed to make unavailability of a single system component transparent to the end user.

Grid Computing – an architecture that allows computing power to be used as if it were a utility. Multiple systems comprise the grid, and individual systems can be added, removed, and upgraded without affecting the grid as a whole.

High availability – maximizing availability of information systems that are mission critical to an organization.

Hot-cold site – a DRP configuration in which the primary site is up and running for normal operations (hot) and the cold DRP site is preconfigured but shut down and not kept in synch with the primary. Tape backups from the primary can be shipped to the cold site but they are not applied. In the event of disaster, the cold site receives the most recent copy of tapes available

Hot-hot site – a DRP configuration in which the DRP site is kept up, running, and in constant data synchronization with the current production site. Automatic data transfer from the primary to the DRP site occurs at all times to keep the data in synch. This allows for a near-immediate failover in the event the DRP needs to be executed.

Hot backup – a system or database backup taken while running and available to end users.

ISO-9000 – a standard for management processes and organization that support the best practices in quality workmanship. This ensures the development and release of quality systems.

Life Cycle Management (LCM) – the act of establishing management policies and procedures, design, development, deployment, operation and maintenance, enhancement, and retirement of a system. Life cycle management provides a proactive ingredient to creating, maintaining, enhancing, and ending an HA implementation.

Load balancer – a network device used to balance network traffic sent to system components, enabling optimal performance.

Offline backup – a system or database backup taken while shut down and unavailable to end users.

On-Demand Computing – an architecture in which processing is spread across multiple computers, so that if one fails, another will pick up the load.

Online backup – a system or database backup taken while running and available to end users.

Parallel Computing – a configuration in which clustered computers work together to accomplish individual tasks.

Project Management Planning (PMP) – a group of concepts used for control, leadership, teamwork, and resource management that helps create a successful project. Effective project management planning is a management concept that can assist in achieving highly available systems.

RAID (Redundant Array of Inexpensive/Independent Disks) – a method for managing individual disk storage devices to deliver low cost, high performance, and highly available data.

Secondary database – a database that is kept in sync with the primary database, and stands ready for activation in the event the primary database fails.

Service Continuity Management (SCM) – an approach to maintaining continuity of service.

Service level agreement (SLA) – a document that outlines the levels of systems support necessary to meet business needs and how support will be measured. An SLA may be utilized internally or externally. Internally, the document creates accountability for the IT department, and an external SLA defines deliverables promised by a vendor.

Service Level Management (SLM) – a process of delivering and maintaining IT services. Service requirements are identified to calculate the service level and the cost to maintain that level. Once a service level analysis is complete, a level of service can be established and agreed upon between the customer and service provider in the form of a Service Level Agreement (SLA). Procedures are then constructed to support the SLA.

Single point of failure – a single avenue from one system component to another. If removed, unavailability occurs. For mission-critical information systems, it is important to identify all possible single points of failure. Once identified, the single point of failure should be addressed.

Six Sigma – a disciplined approach and methodology for eliminating defects in any process. It is a measurement of quality that strives for near perfection.

Storage Area Network (SAN) – two or more servers that share a common set of disks, with each server having its own memory and CPU resources.

Synchronous data transfer – transferring data from one source to multiple sources simultaneously.

Transaction logs – a history of transactions or changes to data that is automatically kept by a database. Transaction logs are used for hot backups and after a failure to recover data that changed since the last backup. Transaction logs facilitate point in time recovery.

INDEX

Absolute 8
Accidental manmade disasters 86
active configuration 42
active-active 17, 19, 64
active-passive 17, 18, 64
administrator. 15, 22, 30, 52, 54, 127
Adobe PDF 45
alerting 66, 69, 79
Alterpoint 64
America's Argonne National
  Laboratory 118
anti-terrorism 113
Apache 47
ApacheTomcat 17
Apple 23
application failure 104
Application Server 46, 48, 52, 156
application servers. ii, 17, 18, 21, 24,
  35, 42, 45, 47, 49, 50, 51, 52, 54,
  56, 65, 66, 123
applications 6, 11, 16, 17, 19, 22, 24,
  32, 35, 37, 38, 40, 42, 44, 46, 49,
  51, 57, 58, 59, 67, 74, 92, 100,
  110, 144, 145
arson 85
ASA 64
Asynchronous data transfer .. 88, 144
AT&T 61
Automated processes 78
Automatic 37, 91, 145
automatic transparent failover 32
Automation 78
availability . ii, 2, 4, 5, 7, 8, 9, 10, 11,
  13, 14, 15, 24, 25, 26, 28, 31, 36,
  38, 44, 45, 49, 58, 59, 60, 62, 65,
  66, 67, 69, 70, 71, 75, 76, 78, 79,
  81, 82, 96, 98, 99, 102, 105, 114,
  120, 134, 136, 141, 145, 156
Backup.. 11, 28, 29, 31, 81, 111, 138
backup and recovery .. 10, 12, 20, 28,
  30, 31, 32, 35, 44
backup tapes 90, 91, 93
Backups 11
bandwidth 63, 70

BEA Weblogic 17
blades 63
BlueCat Adonis 67
bomb 85
bug 28, 73
business data 11, 26
caching server 55, 56
Capability Maturity Model ... 74, 144
Capacity Management 74
Carl Kesselman 118
Central Processing Unit 13
change management 73
chassis 63
chassis switches 63
Checkpoint 64
Cisco 63, 64
Citrix servers 66
client satisfaction 2, 35
cluster 15, 16, 17, 18, 19, 24, 25, 38,
  40, 42, 51, 52, 53, 54, 57, 62, 76,
  118, 123, 144
cluster configuration 40
clustered database 36, 37, 38, 39, 40,
  41, 44, 76
Clustered Database Environments 36
Clustered Web Application Servers
  51
clusters 17, 38, 117
Cold 29, 91, 144
cold site 90, 91, 145
Communication 80, 101
competitive advantage 2
confidentiality 59
Configuration 64, 73, 144
Configuration management 64
contingency plan 7, 8, 70
continuity 28, 72, 80, 146
Continuity of Operations Plan 83,
  144
COOP 83, 144
cost management 73
CPU 13, 14, 15, 50, 118, 147
critical database 2, 44, 88

150

critical systems .. 2, 9, 10, 23, 25, 75, 78, 86, 100, 101, 103, 104, 107, 110, 112, 121, 128
CRM 101, 132
Customers 5, 27, 98, 111
Data blocks 19, 20
Data Blocks 20
data concurrency 87, 89, 90, 95
data growth 37, 74, 144
data integrity 113
data replication 87, 88
data storage 19, 26, 37, 104
data warehouses 29
database failure 104
database instances 36, 42
database replication 88
database server 19, 35, 36, 42, 88
database servers ... 15, 23, 36, 41, 42, 51
database transition log files 28
databases 6, 11, 18, 20, 24, 27, 28, 29, 30, 31, 39, 40, 41, 42, 45, 47, 57, 59, 65, 87, 88, 144
Dataguard 33, 34
DB2/UDB 36
Demilitarized Zones 62
Development 87, 101, 108, 109, 111, 156
direct loss 107
disaster recovery plan 10, 85, 89, 144
Disaster Recovery Plan .. ii, 3, 11, 35, 89, 132, 140, 145
Disaster Recovery Planning .. 21, 35, 83
disgruntled employee 86
disk 13, 14, 15, 16, 18, 19, 20, 21, 29, 30, 37, 38, 51, 85, 87, 88, 93, 118, 122, 146
disk management software 19
disk mirroring technologies 87
Distributed Computing 117, 145
DMZ 62, 66, 132
DNS 60, 67, 68, 93, 132, 145
Documentation 81, 141
documents 45, 55, 81, 94, 144
Dr. Ian Foster 118
DRPii, 10, 11, 35, 83, 84, 85, 86, 87, 88, 89, 90, 91, 92, 93, 94, 95, 104, 111, 132, 140, 141, 145
DRP document 86, 94
DRP exercise 94
DRP site 89, 90, 91, 92, 93, 94, 104, 145
DRP sites 88
DRP walk through 94
dual core technology 14
earthquake 84
eCommerce 6, 101
Email 107
EMC 21
End users 27, 98, 104, 111
Environmental disasters 84
ERP 101
failover ii, 17, 18, 32, 42, 52, 53, 56, 64, 91, 93, 112, 126, 144, 145
failure ii, 5, 7, 12, 13, 14, 15, 16, 17, 18, 19, 20, 24, 25, 27, 28, 29, 30, 31, 32, 34, 35, 36, 40, 42, 44, 49, 52, 73, 76, 83, 84, 85, 88, 104, 108, 109, 110, 112, 113, 122, 124, 126, 127, 138, 144, 145, 147
fault tolerance 14, 19, 20, 32, 36, 49, 50, 51, 53, 57, 76, 122, 124
fault-tolerant 14, 32
Fault-tolerant systems 50, 51
FDA 115
Financial 35, 101, 108
financial impact 99, 101
Firewalls 60, 64
flood 64, 84
Food and Drug Administration ... 115
geographic location 38, 89
Grid Computing 118, 145
HA Accountability 110
HA investment 11, 103, 105, 112
HA management procedures 81
HA planning . 3, 9, 61, 81, 87, 97, 98
hacker 86
hardware ii, 6, 11, 13, 14, 15, 17, 19, 21, 22, 23, 24, 25, 26, 27, 32, 35, 38, 39, 51, 55, 60, 63, 64, 67, 69, 72, 73, 79, 84, 85, 87, 88, 89, 90, 92, 93, 104, 117, 124

Hardware Cluster Architecture 15
Hardware Considerations 14
hardware failure 104
Health Insurance Portability and
    Accountability Act 114
high-end server computing 22
HIPAA 114
Hitachi 21
Hitachi Data Systems 21
horizontal scaling 19, 36, 50
Horizontal scaling 36
Hot 29, 63, 91, 92, 145
hot replaceable components 13
hot-cold 90, 92
hot-cold site 90
hot-hot 90, 91, 92, 95
hot-hot site 91
hours of support 99, 136
HP 22
HR 101
HTML 45, 55, 56, 144
human error 39
hurricane 84
IBM 22, 36
indirect losses 107
InfoBlox 67
Integrated computer systems 27
Integrity 60
Intel 24
Internet. ii, 14, 45, 54, 58, 60, 61, 62,
    64, 67, 68, 69, 70, 85, 104, 120,
    125, 132, 138, 145
Internet Connectivity 60
Internet service provider 61, 104
intrusion prevention 66
ISO-9000 .... 75, 145
ISP 61, 67, 132
Java application 48
Java Virtual Machine 48
Juniper Netscreen 64
JVM 48
Knowledge Transfer 80
large-scale disasters 90
LCM 73, 74, 146
LDAP 63
legacy systems 21
legal penalties 35

Life Cycle Management 73
Linux .. 14, 23, 24, 67, 117, 123, 156
Linux clusters 117
load balancing .... ii, 42, 52, 53, 62
load-balancing algorithms 53
logging 30, 60, 63, 69
logs 30, 33, 34, 42, 147
Mac OS 23
Mainframe 21
man hours 101, 107, 109, 112
Management ii, 4, 27, 61, 68, 71, 72,
    73, 74, 101, 111, 122, 132, 136,
    144, 146
management process 71
Managing HA 10, 71, 78
Managing Memory Synchronization
    38
Manmade disasters 85
memory . 13, 15, 38, 40, 50, 55, 117,
    118, 147
memory management 38
Methodologies 71
Microsoft Windows 21, 23
Microsoft Word 45
Mirrored systems 117, 118
mirroring 15, 20, 37, 87, 88
Mirroring 15
Mitigating Risk 103
monitoring 61, 63, 68, 69, 78, 79, 80,
    102, 104, 108, 126, 127, 128, 129,
    136
MRTG 69
multi-node clustered environment 40
NAC 60
national security 113
natural disaster 7, 105
natural disasters 83, 84
Network Admission Control 60
Network Attached Storage 20
network computing 23
network connections 6, 27, 63
network design 64
network failure 104
Network Load Balancing 54
Network management 60
network operations center 68
Network Security 64

152

network utilization 63
NOC 68, 70, 132
offline backup 29
On-Demand Computing 118, 146
online backup 29
Operating Systems 13, 21, 36
OPS 118
optimize 38
Oracle Corporation 32, 33, 34, 36
Oracle instances 40
Oracle's parallel system 118
Orion 69
outsource 70, 75, 79, 80
outsourcing 9, 68, 80
Parallel Computing 117, 146
partitioning 36
passive standby mode 42
patching 67
Payroll 100, 101
performance. ii, 2, 12, 14, 15, 19, 20,
  25, 29, 36, 37, 38, 40, 47, 51, 53,
  56, 58, 61, 70, 73, 79, 88, 94, 98,
  124, 126, 136, 144, 146
performance capacity 88
Pix 64
PMP 73, 74, 146
portals 46
power failure 6, 7, 28, 104
Power sources 27, 138
power supply 6, 11, 85
proactive monitoring 78
Production 86, 101, 111
production system 79, 85, 87, 102,
  105
program error 28
quality assurance 73
Qwest 61
RAC 36, 40, 118, 132
RAID 19, 20, 36, 37, 132, 146
Reactive support 78
Real Application Clusters 36, 40,
  118, 132
recover. 7, 16, 17, 24, 29, 30, 31, 35,
  83, 85, 86, 87, 147
recoverability 11, 29, 31, 38

redundancy .. ii, 5, 11, 13, 16, 36, 37,
  42, 49, 54, 57, 59, 60, 61, 91, 122,
  144
Redundant Array of
  Inexpensive/Independent Disks19,
  146
Redundant Web Application Servers
  .... 49, 50
Regulatory Compliance 113
regulatory laws 113
remote administration 9
reporting 61, 67, 69, 134, 136
Required Availability 8
Return on Investment 112
risk5, 31, 71, 73, 75, 96, 97, 98, 101,
  103, 104, 105, 106, 110, 112, 126
ROI 110, 112
roll back transactions 30
routers 27, 59, 61, 63, 69
Routine maintenance 49, 78, 79
Routing 62
sabotage 104
SAN environment 16
SAN environments 16
scalability 17, 22, 37, 51, 58
scheduled downtime 7
SCM 72, 74, 132, 146
SEC 115
Secondary Database Environments
  32
Secure Sockets Layer 46
Securities and Exchange
  Commission 115
security ii, 28, 58, 59, 60, 61, 64, 70,
  76, 86, 93, 100, 101, 104, 116
Security 79, 101, 111, 140
Service benchmarks 99
Service Continuity 72, 132, 146
service level agreement 10
Service Level Agreement .. 3, 12, 73,
  77, 132, 134, 136, 147
Shadow Image 21
shared data source 41
single point of failure 5, 6, 13, 24,
  37, 147
Six Sigma 74, 147

153

SLA ... 10, 12, 13, 14, 15, 25, 44, 61, 68, 73, 74, 77, 79, 81, 95, 98, 99, 112, 132, 134, 146, 147
software . 5, 6, 11, 13, 14, 16, 17, 18, 19, 20, 22, 23, 24, 25, 26, 27, 28, 29, 30, 32, 38, 39, 40, 44, 47, 48, 49, 51, 54, 55, 69, 72, 73, 79, 86, 87, 93, 104, 109, 115, 117, 118, 124, 125, 126
Solar Winds 69
Sprint 61
SSL 46
Stakeholder 11, 97, 98
stakeholder buy-in 11, 97, 104
standby 32, 33, 34, 35, 38, 42, 63, 87, 88, 93, 118
standby database 32, 33, 34, 35
standby system 42
Storage Area Network ... 15, 16, 132, 147
Storage Array Networks 20
Storage Management 13, 19, 37
striping 20
Sun 22, 118
switches 27, 59, 63, 138
Switching 42, 62
switchover 34
Symmetric Remote Data Facility .. 21
synchronization .. 38, 39, 42, 91, 123, 145
Synchronous data transfer 88, 147
syslog 64
system failure 7, 14, 17
System infrastructure diagram 81
tabletop exercise 94

Tape backups 88, 90, 145
text files 45
theft 60, 104
throughput 36, 42, 63, 93
time management 73
Tomcat 66
tornado 84, 94
transaction 28, 30, 33, 34, 40, 51
Transition 80, 81
Transition plan 81
TrueCopy 21
UNIX . 14, 21, 22, 23, 24, 67, 75, 76, 85
unscheduled downtime 7
uptime 2, 8, 16, 17, 19, 24, 78
user application requests 41
user error 7, 28
User error 104
Vandalism 104
vertical scaling 50
Virtual Router Redundancy protocol 63
virus 28, 65, 66
VRRP 63
WAN 35, 69
web application servers 50, 51
web browser 48
web computing environment 51, 120
Web Server 45
web site unavailability 107
Websphere 66
What's Up Gold 69
Wide Area Network 35
Windows Enterprise Server 118
worldwide users 58

OTHER BOOKS BY PERPETUAL TECHNOLOGIES' EXPERTS

Look for availability at your favorite bookstore.

- SQL Functions Programmer's Reference
- Database Design
- Teach Yourself Beginning Databases in 24 Hours
- Teach Yourself SQL in 21 Days, 4th Edition
- Teach Yourself SQL in 24 Hours, 3rd Edition
- Oracle 8 Server Unleashed
- Oracle Development Unleashed
- Oracle Unleashed, 2nd Edition
- Oracle DBA on Unix and Linux
- Oracle 10g Application Server
- Unix Primer Plus

Contact Us

Visit us on the web for additional information about high availability and other technical resources. If you would like to request a complimentary copy of our 20-page white paper to learn how Remote Database Administration can save your organization money and increase availability, please call (800) 538-0453 or visit www..perptech.com.

www.perptech.com

Made in the USA